Palgrave Studies in Music and Literature

Series Editors
Paul Lumsden
City Centre Campus
MacEwan University
Edmonton, AB, Canada

Marco Katz Montiel
Facultad de Letras
Pontifical Catholic University of Chile
Santiago, RM - Santiago, Chile

This leading-edge series joins two disciplines in an exploration of how music and literature confront each other as dissonant antagonists while also functioning as consonant companions. By establishing a critical connection between literature and music, this series highlights the interaction between what we read and hear. Investigating the influence music has on narrative through history, theory, culture, or global perspectives provides a concrete framework for a seemingly abstract arena. Titles in the series, both monographs and edited volumes, explore musical encounters in novels and poetry, considerations of the ways in which narratives appropriate musical structures, examinations of musical form and function, and studies of interactions with sound.

More information about this series at
http://www.palgrave.com/gp/series/15596

Angus Cleghorn
Editor

Elizabeth Bishop and the Music of Literature

palgrave
macmillan

Editor
Angus Cleghorn
Seneca College
Toronto, ON, Canada

Palgrave Studies in Music and Literature
ISBN 978-3-030-33179-5   ISBN 978-3-030-33180-1   (eBook)
https://doi.org/10.1007/978-3-030-33180-1

Cover illustration: Petr Bonek / Alamy Stock Photo

This Palgrave Pivot imprint is published by the registered company Springer Nature Switzerland AG.
The registered company address is: Gewerbestrasse 11, 6330 Cham, Switzerland

.

Elizabeth Bishop and the Grateful Dead
(San Francisco, 1968–1969)
by Jeffrey Harrison

Whether she ever saw them perform we don't know,
but she did go to a Janis Joplin show,
and Thom Gunn's account of smoking a joint with her
backstage at a group reading makes it easier
to imagine her chatting with Jerry during a break
(about Billie Holliday, or Baudelaire, or Blake)
if not dancing in the aisles during one of the band's
already notoriously labyrinthine jams,
like the one between "Dark Star" and "Saint Stephen"
(a new song in their repertoire that season).
He would have been twenty-six, she fifty-seven.
She might have let it drop that Donovan
wanted to record "The Burglar of Babylon,"
he might have praised her trippy "Riverman,"
but she probably wouldn't have uttered the phrase
she'd used in one of her unfinished essays
to describe the music of a rock band she'd seen
several times that year: a fucking machine—
though that might have led to a flurry of wit
or perhaps a killer rendition of "Love Light,"
with Pigpen lewdly rapping, in the second set.
Unlikely? Still, I'd like to think it happened—

my favorite poet meeting my favorite band.
Her partner then was in her twenties and
had connections to the music scene. Also,
in the year and a half she lived in San Francisco,
the Dead gave over sixty-five performances
so you'd think she'd have seen them once. Is
that too much of a stretch? Well, this just in:
five or so years later, on one of her trips up
to her beloved Nova Scotia, Bishop
brought as a present for her teenage cousin
a copy of *Europe '72*—a triple album
gathered from live concerts—telling him
the Grateful Dead was a band to know about ...
and also that it was okay to smoke pot.

ACKNOWLEDGMENTS

Thanks to the Elizabeth Bishop Society and the American Literature Association for hosting two panels on "Voice, Tone, and Music" at the 2017 annual conference in Boston. Six papers formed the core of this book, which was developed with the encouragement of Palgrave Macmillan's Allie Troyanos and external readers who provided valuable critical insights. Thomas Travisano and Jonathan Ellis provided helpful assistance in the book's development. Thanks to Rachel Jacobe for her editorial work and to the authors of this book for their expertise and patience. I am grateful to Claire Moane and the School of English and Liberal Studies at Seneca College in Toronto for supporting my conference participation and collaborations with Bishop scholars. Thanks also to my family—Julie, Andrew, and Simon—for enabling study time and providing vital energies together. Let me not forget my parents and sisters, who shared a house of music.

Elizabeth Bishop and the Grateful Dead was first published in *The Yale Review*, © Jeffrey Harrison. Used with permission of the author.

Lisa Goldfarb's chapter, "Music of the Sea: Elizabeth Bishop and Symbolist Poetics," is based on a longer version of "Bishop and the Symbolists" in Chapter V of her book, *Unexpected Affinities: Modern American Poetry and Symbolist Poetics*, published by Sussex Academic Press. Goldfarb is grateful to the editor for acknowledging and agreeing to the publication of this current chapter. Thanks to Sussex Academic Press for permission.

Quotations from the unpublished writings of Elizabeth Bishop are used with the permission of Archives and Special Collections, Vassar College Library. Excerpts of the unpublished notes are printed with permission of Farrar, Straus, and Giroux, LLC on behalf of the Elizabeth Bishop Estate.

CONTENTS

NOTES ON CONTRIBUTORS

Angus Cleghorn is Professor of English and Liberal Studies at Seneca College, Toronto, Canada. He has coedited *The Cambridge Companion to Elizabeth Bishop* (2014), *Elizabeth Bishop in the Twenty-First-Century: Reading the New Editions* (2012); authored *Wallace Stevens' Poetics: The Neglected Rhetoric* (2000); and written numerous essays on Stevens and Bishop.

Andrew Eastman is a Senior Lecturer in the Department of Anglophone Studies at the University of Strasbourg, France. He has published numerous articles on rhythm and subjectivity in the twentieth-century poetry, and is working on a book focusing on modernist rhythm and rhyme.

Lisa Goldfarb is a professor at the Gallatin School of New York University, president of The Wallace Stevens Society, and an associate editor of *The Wallace Stevens Journal*. She is the author of *Unexpected Affinities: Modern American Poetry and Symbolist Poetics* (2018) and *The Figure Concealed: Wallace Stevens, Music, and Valéryan Echoes* (2011). She is also the coeditor of *Wallace Stevens, New York, and Modernism* (2012); *Poetry and Poetics after Wallace Stevens* (2017); and *Wallace Stevens, Poetry, and France: "Au pays de la métaphore"* (2017).

Maria Lúcia Milléo Martins is a full professor in the English Department of Universidade Federal de Santa Catarina, Brazil. She has written *Antologia de Poesia Norte-Americana Contemporânea* (as translator), *Duas Artes: Carlos Drummond de Andrade e Elizabeth Bishop*, and several essays in the area of poetry. Her most recent study, *Poesia Canadense Contemporânea e Multiculturalismo*, is forthcoming soon.

Deryn Rees-Jones is a poet, editor, and critic. Her critical work has focused on the work of twentieth- and twenty-first-century women's writing, including *Consorting with Angels* and the accompanying anthology *Modern Women Poets* (2005). *Paula Rego: The Art of Story*, *Erato*, and *Fires* are all published in 2019. She is the editor of the Pavilion Poetry series for Liverpool University Press.

Lloyd Schwartz is Frederick S. Troy Professor of English at University of Massachusetts, Boston, USA, and a commentator on music and the arts for National Public Radio's *Fresh Air*, the web journal *New York Arts*, and WBUR's *The ARTery*. As the Classical Music Editor of *The Boston Phoenix*, he was awarded the 1994 Pulitzer Prize for Criticism. He is the author of four books of poetry, most recently *Little Kisses*, and is one of Elizabeth Bishop's major editors: *Elizabeth Bishop and Her Art*; *Elizabeth Bishop: Poems, Prose, and Letters*; and the centennial edition of Elizabeth Bishop's *Prose*.

Christopher Spaide is a lecturer in the Department of English at Harvard University, USA. His articles on modern and contemporary American poetry have appeared or are forthcoming in *The Cambridge Quarterly*, *College Literature*, *Contemporary Literature*, and *Poetry*.

Yuki Tanaka teaches at Hosei University, Japan. He holds an MFA in Poetry from the Michener Center for Writers at the University of Texas-Austin, and a Ph.D. in English from Washington University, St. Louis.

Thomas Travisano is Professor Emeritus at Hartwick College, USA. He is the author of *Love Unknown: The Life and Worlds of Elizabeth Bishop*, *Elizabeth Bishop: Her Artistic Development* and *Midcentury Quartet: Bishop, Lowell, Jarrell, Berryman, and the Making of a Postmodern Aesthetic*. He served as principal editor of *Words in Air: The Complete Correspondence Between Elizabeth Bishop and Robert Lowell* and coeditor of *Gendered Modernisms: American Women Poets and Their Readers*, *Elizabeth Bishop in the Twenty-First Century: Reading the New Editions*, and the three-volume The New Anthology of American Poetry. He is the founding president of the Elizabeth Bishop Society.

Abbreviations[1]

EAP   *Edgar Allan Poe & the Juke-Box: Uncollected Poems, Drafts, and Fragments.* Ed. Alice Quinn. New York: Farrar, Straus and Giroux, 2006.

OA   *One Art: Letters.* Ed. Robert Giroux. NY: Farrar, Straus, Giroux, 1994.

P   *Poems.* New York: Farrar, Straus, Giroux, 2011.

PPL   Bishop, Elizabeth. *Poems, Prose, and Letters.* Eds. Lloyd Schwartz and Robert Giroux. New York: Library of America, 2008.

Pr   *Prose.* Ed. Lloyd Schwartz. New York: Farrar, Straus, Giroux, 2011.

VA   Elizabeth Bishop Collection. Vassar College Library. Poughkeepsie, New York.

WIA   Elizabeth Bishop and Robert Lowell. *Words in Air: The Complete Correspondence Between Elizabeth Bishop and Robert Lowell.* Edited by Thomas Travisano with Saskia Hamilton. New York: Farrar, Straus and Giroux, 2008.

Note

1. Unless otherwise indicated, literature discussed in this volume is from Elizabeth Bishop, *Poems, Prose, and Letters,* edited by Lloyd Schwartz and Robert Giroux (New York: Library of America, 2008).

CHAPTER 1

Introduction

Angus Cleghorn

Abstract Spaces form chambers for Elizabeth Bishop's music. Sounds reverberate from the pages of Bishop's poetry, often overtly displaying their sound patterns to readers, while simultaneously intoning external soundscapes. The chapters in this volume meticulously display Bishop's virtuosity with transforming traditional poetic and musical forms into her own innovative adaptations fitting contemporary experience. Seemingly natural voices become our own in poems that also register dissonances of others. This leads readers to consider cultural conflicts, exclamations both humorous and violent, that ask us to reconsider our contextual living conditions. Beyond playful interrogations of how linguistic sounds define us and what we know, Bishop provides a fluid range of tones to explore difference. Her poetic music from European and North American traditions extends to twentieth-century Brazilian genres. Furthermore, her literature's musical settings have inspired diverse scores by twentieth-century composers and current songwriters around the globe.

Keywords Bishop • Music • Chamber • Voice • Tone • Rhythm

A. Cleghorn (✉)
Seneca College, Toronto, ON, Canada

© The Author(s) 2019
A. Cleghorn (ed.), *Elizabeth Bishop and the Music of Literature*,
Palgrave Studies in Music and Literature,
https://doi.org/10.1007/978-3-030-33180-1_1

1

Whether it be a village, church, ballroom, house with a clavichord, apartment, seashore or poem, spaces form chambers for Elizabeth Bishop's music. In *The Making of a Poem*, Mark Strand and Eavan Boland project this idea while discussing "One Art":

> it turns around and around, building an acoustic chamber for the words, the lines, the meanings: *The art of losing isn't hard to master.* As the villanelle gathers strength and speed, this coda—*the art of losing*—moves in and out of irony, grief, self-accusation, regret. … This effect of the villanelle—to make an acoustic chamber for single words—was particularly well understood by Bishop. (20)

This sonic chamber (an abode for the mouth) is the forum in which this book reverberates. The lead chapter by Deryn Rees-Jones on Bishop's clavichord makes use of this instrument as a domestic companion that mediates between inner and outer worlds, and thereby transforms emotion into harmony. Bishop's poems resound in readers so that they become our own. Voices inside our heads become treasures "living in the cave of the mouth," as Robert Frost put it (Cook 223). How the poet manages to achieve this is on the one hand simple, for every decent poet does it, yet Bishop does it with such diverse and dazzling virtuosity that the poems firmly stick; they register so strongly that we need to look into their adherences further.

Eleanor Cook prompts this quest in *Elizabeth Bishop at Work* with "curiosity about exactly how she did it, this master poet of the twentieth century" (1). And in her chapter eight, it's the slippery notion of tone that Cook identifies as perhaps the most difficult register to describe and understand. "She can alter the dominant tone like a musician. She can shift tones very quietly within a poem, like the slight altering of a repeating phrase in music. Or she can change tone *fortissimo*, like a change of key in music" (225). This book grew partly from Cook's challenge as developed in an American Literature Association (ALA) conference double panel on "Voice, Tone and Music in Elizabeth Bishop's Writing" in Boston, in May 2017. Two of the papers focused on "At the Fishhouses." The musical and tonal diversity of this masterpiece was cast in the Symbolist poetic tradition by Lisa Goldfarb, who employs Baudelaire, Rimbaud and particularly Valéry's musical poetics to observe Bishop's distinct valences. Then in a meticulous, close reading of the same poem, Yuki Tanaka studies syntactic rhythms to reveal the poetic dynamics of unfolding emotional drama. A similarly acute ear from Andrew Eastman is "Hearing Things in Bishop," this time through reverberations of others' voices that echo her own voice as it comes back to her, and by sounding other voices the poem makes a place for the reader's voice to emerge. This book's movement from inner to outer voices becomes a cacophony in Christopher Spaide's "Causes for Excess: Elizabeth Bishop's Eighty-Eight Exclamations," in which her inimitable voice depends on the occasional excess that, paradoxically, arrives only in precisely controlled circumstances. Spaide takes note of how vocal practice changes throughout her career. My chapter focuses on "Voice Control in Late Bishop" to show how her poetry develops prosaic utterances to disrupt musical harmony and thereby offer disjunctive cultural commentary through rhetorical voices with recognizable signals for readers.

This book unsettles Bishop's old reputation for quiet reserve. Thomas Travisano charts "A Very Important Violence of Tone" in "Roosters" and other poems. From her early verses and prose to late lyrics, Bishop carefully prepares for moments of violence that flash out from a seemingly calm or settled verbal environment. Physical place is always key—from Newfoundland in "The Map" and "Cape Breton" in that Nova Scotian poem to the startling geographical range found in Brazil. Maria Lúcia Milléo Martins attends to "Bishop and Brazilian popular music: from anonymous sambas to contemporary composers." In Brazil Bishop wrote, "I suspect [sambas] are some of the last folk poetry to be made in the world," and this study discusses the cultural and political implications, and resonances of Brazilian popular lyrical forms such as cordel, choro and bossa nova in her own poetry. Lloyd Schwartz extends Bishop's music further by showing how her diverse musical settings have inspired global contemporary composers in an array of musical genres. By the end of this small book we will notice huge range from Bishop's youthful and internal "need for music," her wandering cultural outreach and the numerous reverberations from musicians paying tribute to her ear through theirs.

Bishop's early musical foundation was made from the hymns she sang and heard in Great Village, Nova Scotia, piano and harmony lessons at Walnut Hill School in Massachusetts, as well as her studies at Vassar College in Poughkeepsie, New York, where she planned to major in music and took a senior course in Music as a Literature (Marshall 36), which inspired this book's title. Bishop's reading of other poets cannot be underestimated in her carefully formed ear, and experiments with formal poetics from sestinas to sonnets to Romantic ballads to the sprung rhythms of Hopkins, prose poems of Baudelaire, Rimbaud and Stein, the innovative

Modernist techniques of Eliot, Stevens, Moore and Auden, as well as contemporaries such as Swenson, Lowell and Rich. See Bonnie Costello's chapter on "Bishop and the Poetic Tradition" in *The Cambridge Companion to Elizabeth Bishop* for thorough exploration. In her adulthood, Bishop listened to the blues-jazz of Billie Holiday, Brazilian sambas, the folk songs of Bob Dylan and the Grateful Dead, and in the 1970s she attended orchestral concerts and chamber music by the likes of Elliott Carter in Boston.

Many tones spring from Bishop's poetry. Her voice manages to control them so tightly that as readers we are sometimes taken aback by the musical interpretations of others, whether that may be a complex modern composition or just a different extrapolation from another reader. As Gillian White has written, Bishop creates "space in art" where together we can hear things. And yet we may hear different things. As Rachel Trousdale suggests in a forthcoming essay on humor, one reader will hear "Filling Station" as crude class snobbery, while another will register love. Bishop's tones enable us to see both perspectives and more, as Trousdale explains in a paper recently presented at the 2019 ALA annual conference in Boston:

> Her humorous asides, wry ironies, and satirical critiques help her hold competing ideas in double exposure: her levity presents varying viewpoints without necessarily taking sides. Her humor fuses empathy with judgment, as her subjects' and speakers' frailties are to be both rejected and felt as our own.

In the case of "Filling Station," some readers identify with the greasy family, others laugh along with the speaker's snobby judgments, and others do both. The poem itself appears to form this latter kind of fusion with its last words, "Somebody loves us all" (*PPL* 123).

The mystery is how accurately Bishop's words ring spontaneously in our heads. It is different music from the steady sonorities of Yeats, the philosophical meditations comically punctuated by Stevens, the busy clamor of Eliot's polyphony or the firm control of Moore. I suggest that we hear Bishop's music in a more pronounced way that sticks in the ear largely because of her careful narrative guidance. The poetic voice takes readers into "The Map" so that "[w]e can stroke these lovely bays," and the same reliable narrator gradually and momentarily morphs into "the printer here experiencing the same excitement / as when emotion too far exceeds its cause" (*PPL* 3). This storytelling leads us on a stroll of the map's tactile peninsulas grasped "between thumb and finger / like women feeling for the smoothness of yard-goods." In a way, Bishop's poetic narrators resemble Whitman hooking the waist of the reader so he can point to democratic vistas and new horizons. Moreover, Bishop often amalgamates the senses into a synesthesia of bodily music that is felt and conceptualized simultaneously. Yet this power is fleeting and provisional, often through her use of simile, but also due to her modulating, revisory narrators. In "The Map," just after we feel "the smoothness of yard-goods," the next stanza begins with an intellectual step back from sensory immersion so that we trust the balanced narrator: "Mapped waters are more quiet than the land is," and it almost does not matter whether her actual statement makes sense; the authorial tone has us believe it. We become pawns for her voice to lead us through the land and water of "The Map" on which "Norway's hare runs south in agitation," which is comic fancy we can picture.

Similar modulations permeate the narrative of "The Monument," which we view from the tour guide and tourist's voices until the old statuary form is deconstructed so we can begin to put it back together again—as any evolving artform. Music here is not just what we hear from the voices; it's in the undulating, modulating, revising, adding, subtracting, qualifying, asserting and demonstrating. Bishop goes a step further than Stevens' "poem in the act of the mind" by taking the poem out of the mind to see it functioning in the social world, in addition to the many other epistemological arenas. This is especially the case in the opening poems of *Questions of Travel*, which, like "The Monument," perform dialogic explorations—this time touring through Brazilian geography, culture, maps and history. As a complete volume, including the "Elsewhere" of Nova Scotia, *Questions of Travel* is a myriad display of voices revealing Bishop's musical registration of place and people.

Music is a mode, an abode and instrumental in Bishop's innovative contribution to poetry. The lyric is a musical genre that has traditionally presented solo songs of soul. For Bishop, this base is enriched by multiple voices of self and others ringing within and clanging outside. In the following chapters, we will see how her work artfully registers itself through form, and through the rhythms of culture reverberating in our ears.

CHAPTER 2

"I am in Need of Music": Elizabeth Bishop and the Energies of Sound and Song

Deryn Rees-Jones

Abstract Using the narrative of Bishop's ongoing interest in music, evidenced in her early musical notebooks, and in particular her love for the clavichord, this chapter explores Bishop's interest in repetition and rhythm. Focusing on a discussion of her early poem "Anaphora," the chapter shows how Bishop, from an early stage, is using music to develop a social model for the lyric that also allows her to locate and embody herself temporally, and to engage with the unsayable losses of her early years. Several other of Bishop's early poems in *North & South*, which invoke the musical study or song, particularly "Song—for the Clavichord," "Little Exercise" and "Songs for a Colored Singer," are also examined.

Keywords Music • Song • Lyric • Clavichord • Rhythm • Repetition

"Where is the music coming from, the energy?" Elizabeth Bishop asks in "Anaphora" (*PPL* 39–40), a poem published in 1945, and placed with typical precision at the end of her first book, *North & South* (1946). The

D. Rees-Jones (✉)
University of Liverpool, Liverpool, UK

© The Author(s) 2019
A. Cleghorn (ed.), *Elizabeth Bishop and the Music of Literature*,
Palgrave Studies in Music and Literature,
https://doi.org/10.1007/978-3-030-33180-1_2

"music," somehow everywhere but nowhere, unlocatable in its diffuse presence, is a complex blend of sound: the songs of birds, the noise of church bells and "whistles from a factory." Each sound sits in rich counterpoint with the other, offering a symbolically structured mesh as Bishop brings nature, the institutions of religion and the world of work and society together to offer us a soundscape as she explores the possibilities of transforming our inhabitation of the world into a kind of complex form. The musical study, designed to promote technical skills, and as a vehicle of repetition and rhythmical complexity, like the poem, is proposed as the space that will allow the fiery event of the day to take place. The process of negotiation of such energies continued to be explored over the next 30 years in Bishop's writing, reaching a climax in that later great poem "In the Waiting Room" (1977), when the speaker famously announces, in a moment of epiphany, prompted by a particular coalescence of sound and image that allows her to come into a state of being and recognition: "you are an *I,*/you are an Elizabeth" (*PPL* 149–151). But what are these energies? And how do they become so connected to the musical structures that are so central to Bishop's work?

In letters written across her lifetime, Bishop gives accounts of her love for music that range from Scarlatti to Webern, to samba, jazz and popular Brazilian folk music. Yet the importance of music to Bishop's poetics, throughout her writing life, the "energies" she seeks to access and formalize within the structures of the poem, has until recently been largely overlooked in favour of her recourse to the visual. References to music and song are integral to the development of her work, not least because of her reading of the French symbolists, especially Baudelaire, and her own awareness of their influence on Pound, Eliot and Stevens. In her late teens Bishop had seen Myra Hess and Prokofiev perform and Bishop's reading about music even at an early age was wide, something to which the undated bibliography for her 1928 high school essay "Elizabethan Music"—which includes W. S. Bratt's 1907 *The History of Music, The Dictionary of Old Music* (1923) and a collection in German of John Dowland's lute music—bears testimony.[1] "Elizabethan Music" begins by bringing together the sounds of the world with the playing of an instrument, with a charming knowingness that also suggests the laying of preoccupations that will continue to resurface in her desire to pursue her musical studies. "The hucksters are calling their wares through the streets of every town and city with strange and musical cries," she writes, "and Queen Elizabeth is practicing daily on her virginal." Bishop's essay continues to explore a fantasy about relationships between men, women and music, at the centre of which is an Elizabethan wife, who "adopts the popular Elizabeth attitude of melancholy"; her own "beautiful virginal," she notes, has a "leather case to take it travelling in" (VA 69.A1). In a sonnet also drafted in 1928, Bishop writes, "I am in need of music that would flow/Over my fretful, feeling fingertips,/Over my bitter-tainted, trembling lips,/With melody, deep, clear, and liquid-slow," yearning for "the healing swaying, old and low,/Of some song sung to rest the tired dead" (*PPL* 186).

Elsewhere in the manuscripts gathered in the library at Vassar are numerous scrawled fragments about accent, emphasis and rhythm in music; her 1934–1935 notes when she studied clavichord with the young musician Ralph Kirkpatrick are those of someone thinking seriously about playing (VA 71.3). Kirkpatrick had made his debut playing Bach's *Goldberg Variations* on the harpsichord in Berlin, and had trained with the Dolmetsch workshop in England in 1932, a fact that almost certainly strengthened the link in her mind with Pound, music and her own playing. Pound's great hero, Arnold Dolmetsch (1858–1940), had pioneered a revival in early instruments, and was responsible, Pound claimed, for helping poets to break the constraints of regularized form in free verse and for emphasizing through the image of the troubadour, the relationship of poetry and music, claiming that "*vers libre* exists in old music."[2] Writing to Frani Blough in 1935, Bishop had described her playing of the clavichord, which she had taken up, as being "quite suited to my needs," citing Pound's statement: "The further poetry departs from music, the more decadent it gets" (*OA* 31). In this letter she also pronounces her enthusiasm for an article in *Hound & Horn*, which seems to be referring to an article by Roger Pryor Dodge, "Harpsichords and Jazz Trumpets," a now seminal essay on improvisation.[3]

Bishop's decision to pursue her musical studies after her graduation and the death of her mother in 1934 whom she had not seen since she was five, were undoubtedly, if not consciously, also subsequently tightly bound up in the painful circumstances of the years that had followed. Back in New York in 1936 after her first trip to Europe, and living in the Chelsea Hotel, Robert Seaver, the suitor whom she had rejected, killed himself; in 1937, having returned to Paris, Bishop was involved in a car accident in which her close friend the painter Margaret Miller tragically lost her right arm. It was against the backdrop of these three harrowing years, and perhaps aware of her future itinerant life, that in 1937 Bishop made a practical commitment to her musical studies by commissioning her own clavichord from the Dolmetsch workshops, using an inheritance after the death of her Uncle Jack, John Jr. Bishop. The clavichord, which was initially shipped out to her in Paris, was later described by Bishop's friend the pianist and harpsichordist Rosalyn Tureck as "a superb, beautiful instrument of excellent tone and modestly decorated in overall green with gold lettering."[4] Bishop's commissioning of the clavichord not only reflected her tie to Kirkpatrick but also consolidated the link to Pound, and her interest in early music and seventeenth-century poetry, and indeed the later links to Pound, whom she was to visit in St Elizabeths hospital when she was living in Washington as the consultant in poetry to the Library of Congress between 1949 and 1950.[5]

If the purchase of the clavichord was financed by another loss, it also represented a way of transforming that loss. As Brett Millier so astutely points out, the clavichord was to become for Bishop "one of those possessions that is its own reason for being and then organizes and focuses the energy of human beings around it."[6] For months and sometimes years Bishop would lend the clavichord to her friends. On one occasion she nearly gave it away to one musician friend—so ambivalent was she about its return, playfully offering to exchange it for a compass by way of exchange when she eventually collected it. At other points in Bishop's life the clavichord becomes central to order and recovery: she mentions in a letter to Marianne Moore in 1950, as she sadly discusses the death of her psychoanalyst Dr Foster, that it is a pleasure for her that she has her clavichord with her again, although, she says, "she plays it wretchedly" (*OA* 206). Bishop starts to play the clavichord daily, after being hospitalized, because of a five-day drinking bout in Yaddo in the same year. Eventually the clavichord followed her to Brazil in the mid-1950s—it is probably, she writes in another letter, the only clavichord in the whole country; her partner, Lota Soares, comically suggests that she has it electrified, like a guitar. The clavichord simply will not go away, and in exchanges with Anne Stevenson, she very tellingly mentions its existence, alongside discussions of her poem "Anaphora" in 1963 (*PPL* 852). Finally the clavichord accompanies Bishop back to Boston in 1974 before she finally sells it in 1975 to Howard Moss, poet and poetry editor of *The New Yorker*, four years before she died.

Written before she owned her own instrument, like a little poetic wish fulfilment, Bishop's early unfinished draft "Song—for the Clavichord," which Alice Quinn dates at 1935, connects Bishop directly in her writing with a tradition of baroque musical playing. But as a metaphor for the musical impulses in her work, the clavichord itself holds much resonance. Its reputation as a quiet instrument, unsuitable for public performance, which meant that often the French motto "Plus fait douceur que violence" was painted decoratively across it, speaks most obviously to Bishop's own "quiet" poetic tone. As much an instrument of the world, it becomes a psychic metaphor for composition, and an embodiment of feeling through sound; music seems to offer Bishop a structure for and an orientation of feeling. The clavichord's use as a practice or compositional instrument, on which one studied, or improvised, also lends a sense to it as a rather wonderful and even surreal baroque version of the typewriter, as portable as the suitcase, a "domestic instrument," as Pound called it, which allows music to remain in a private space and "home made."[7] For Aristotle, the playing of music performed the function of emotional regulation and processing. And indeed in a letter to Marianne Moore in October 1936, Bishop enthusiastically, if ambivalently, describes her first lesson with Kirkpatrick and how he gave her "all sorts of exercises to do which I feel to be a little overmystical, almost yoga-ish" (*OA* 46). Bishop's perceived failure—her sense of her bad playing—nevertheless seems to simultaneously work itself out as a place of return to something which music can embody for her. Bishop's engagement with the clavichord, via her lessons with Kirkpatrick and her reading of Pound, offer an interesting context for her understanding of poetry's musical structures. It is listening to a recording of Kirkpatrick playing Scarlatti, which she remarks allows her to finish "Roosters" in 1941 (*PPL* 844).

If poetry is the art that Bishop is able to make and "master," playing an instrument (rather than composition of music) seems to settle in her as the place where she cannot quite attain the brilliance or technical mastery it demands of her.

"Song—for the Clavichord" is a love poem that places typical Bishop preoccupations—the dislocated sensibility of the here and there, framed here by love—under the sign of its song: "Love is not here"; she writes:

> He has not gone away;
> He has not found
> A better place to stay.
> He is not places anyway.
>
> He is not old;
> He is not new,
> He is not what you think;
> He is not you,
> Nor you, not you. He's you. (*PPL* 208)

The poem is both *for* the clavichord—a piece that might be played on it—and "for the clavichord" in that it is dedicated to it. With its strange, disorienting search for its addressee, which sees a shift from the pronoun "he" to the direct address of the vocative, it is a poem which has at the back of its mind George Herbert's "Love III." "Love Bade me welcome, yet my soul drew back," begins Herbert's poem, a poem as much about divine encounter as it is about shame and which tellingly contains the line "Love said, You shall be he." The draft for "Song—for the Clavichord," Quinn notes, is in the notebooks placed near another poem draft, "People Who Can't Remember Dreams," later published as "Some Dreams They Forgot," under which Bishop had written in capital letters, TERRIBLE, an exclamation that also contained within it a reference to Hopkins, and his sonnets which she conceded were "terrible" but "short, and in form" (*PPL* 864).[8] Perhaps Bishop also had at the back of her mind Wallace Stevens' "Peter Quince at the Clavier" (1915), a poem in which Stevens draws up a complex analogy between feeling, sound and desire, between the action of the fingers striking the keys in the material world and the world of the perceiving spirit, when he writes: "Music is feeling then, not sound;/And thus it is that what I feel,/Here in this room, desiring you."[9]

How, then, might we begin to link Bishop's use of the clavichord, her poem dedicated to it, and "Anaphora" with its desire for "stupendous studies"? Bishop wrote to the then young poet Anne Stevenson in March 1963 that "Anaphora" was started in Puebla, Mexico, when she was travelling in 1942 with her partner, Marjorie Carr Stevens. It was a fragment from a dream broken as she woke, she explains, "when the cathedral bells clanged just a few yards away from my pillow" (*PPL* 844).[10] Later, writing critically on Bishop, Stevenson reads "Anaphora" as a poem which concerns "death and resurrection of the imagination," a reading which also allies it with a poem on which it also seems to draw, W. B. Yeats' "Sailing to Byzantium," which was published in *The Tower* in 1928.[11] The poem also seems to have embedded into it an ongoing dialogue with Wallace Stevens, and in particular his poems from the 1930s. Bishop was reading Stevens carefully—she knew *Harmonium* (1923), she tells Stevenson, "almost by heart" (*PPL* 862)—but not without some sense of confusion as she negotiated the complexities and inconsistencies of his new work *Owl's Clover* (1936). She confesses to Marianne Moore about the feeling she has of "wandering around them in the dark" (*OA* 48). And although Bishop sees her understanding of Stevens' work of this period as potentially simplistic, she ultimately admires it for its exploration of what she understands as the relationship between poet and poem, of the poet's relationship between "making poetry, the poetry making them" (*OA* 48). The word "energy," which sits slightly oddly in "Anaphora," also seems to recall the philosophical term *energeia* (literally "within work"), which runs in various forms through philosophical thinking from Aristotle to Bergson and Deleuze, and which is, as it is in Bishop's poem, intimately connected to an idea of becoming. Sarah Posman neatly summarizes the changing use of the term, showing how over the centuries it moved from being a term in classical rhetoric suggesting an "enlivened" way of speaking which was to become "a central notion in thinking about the nature of language," to one which saw an energy at work in poetic language which was able to "close the gap between word and things," and "unite speaker and hearer in understanding." It is this which Posman identifies as being at "the heart of a romantic understanding of language."[12] Allying music and energy in the slipped syntactical analogy of the question in "Anaphora"—"Where is the music coming from, the energy?"—Bishop highlights an idea that will continue to thread its way through her oeuvre: that sounds might stand in for what is there—alive and powerful—but which is in some way also unsayable in language. Such a linguistic unsayable becomes instead represented by repeated sounds, patterns, repetitions all signalling a broader desire to enact in that state of becoming an unrecoverable traumatic thought or feeling.[13]

Throughout "Anaphora" Bishop juxtaposes end rhyme with repetition, offering a confusing pattern of sound which moves between order and disorder, connection and its opposite. The double repetition in stanza one of "instantly, instantly falls" across a comma or the repetition of "mortal/ mortal fatigue" across the line break whereby a shift in tone—might I even think semi-tone?—means that the repeated word cries out for a new inflection or accent. Repetition and such uncannily collapsed or floating end rhymes defy a sense of forward expectation that rhyme demands and instead become part of a powerful set of doublings back, and repetitions which reconfigure in a set of parallelisms of the second stanza. But what exactly does the poem remember?

North & South is by any standards a sleep-filled book whose speakers operate in states of reverie, half-awake and half-asleep, seduced and formed by song. Such states of reverie also enact a state that sits in interplay between temporal states, between our conscious and unconscious experiences. In "Dimensions for a Novel" (1934), Bishop writes about "experience-time" in relation to feeling—"We have all had the experience of apparently escaping the emotional results of an event, of feeling no joy or sorrow where joy or sorrow was to be expected"; she writes, continuing:

> If I suffer a terrible loss and do not realize it till several years later among different surroundings, then the important fact is not the original loss so much as the circumstance of the new surroundings which succeeded in letting the loss through to my consciousness. (*PPL* 676–677)

The repetitions and disorientations of "Song—for the Clavichord" are continued in various ways in poems, many of which are located in Paris. The clavichord thus becomes associated for Bishop with the place that is neither here nor there, the past or future, home or away, that she carries both literally and metaphorically around with her.

Anaphora, the repetition of a word or a phrase at the beginning of successive clauses, phrases or sentences, foregrounds a strategy of repetition for rhetorical purposes. Those repetitions place emphasis on a word as a kind of strut to cumulative set of thoughts. But in their repetition those words are also transformed; they become both the same and yet different, working to pulse through a sentence, and, as they accumulate, increasingly to create a space in the text, a kind of memory of what was there so recently and which is now marked by something else. We hear a word, but when we hear it again in such close proximity to itself, it places new emphasis on itself not as meaning but as sound. What these repetitions also offer is a kind of a jam to rhythm, so that the voice must encounter them either dully or through an accentuation that alters the natural rhythm of the line. The last three lines of "Anaphora" are rich in repetition: "the fiery event/of every day in endless/endless assent" also has buried in it the homophone "ascent," a word which is not there but which works again in implicit counterpoint with the falls and falling of all that has come earlier. Set against this unstable rhyme scheme is the poem's rhythm that becomes accentuated through repetition. In particular, Bishop's use of anadiplosis, and her doubling up of the same word next to each other in one sentence, including a use of homonym, emerges throughout her work as a stylistic hallmark. The backward look of the repeated word, its quality of echo, bears testimony not simply to an insistence of the word as thing but also suggests a kind of belatedness of knowing, a belatedness it could be argued which is also echoed in the dedication to Marjorie Carr Stevens, a dedication retrospectively added ten years later. Does that dedication also carry a ghostly, associative memory of her readings of Wallace Stevens during its composition too? It's hard not to notice, as poems are being awarded ownership, that the only other female dedicatee of a poem in the volume is the injured Margaret Miller, in "Quai d'Orléans," a poem that ends with "If what we could see could forget us half as easily" (*PPL* 21).

Bishop is especially thoughtful about the need to create adequate rhythmic structures: "My belief in the peculiar cross-hatchings of events and people also amounts to a feeling for rhythm," she writes (*PPL* 679). Rhythm's timeliness becomes more than an aesthetic choice but involves a negotiation with the past and our means of knowing it. In her undergraduate essay from 1933, "Time's Andromedas," Bishop begins by describing herself reading, as the sun sets, and she becomes aware of the falling light, noting, like the beginning of "Anaphora," a coalescence of the "small sounds" she can hear, "a faintly rhythmic irregularity yet resembling the retreat of innumerable small waves, lake waves, rustling on sand" (*PPL* 641–659). In this essay Bishop goes on to articulate an idea of "the sustained contradictory time-pattern" that is at work when reading. The experience of reading is also the experience of emergence in "Anaphora" whereby consciousness, the coming into being as the poem's speaker wakes, is not about recall and memory but instead attempts to show a complex and dynamic existence, a coexistence of past and present. Both "Song—for the Clavichord" and "Anaphora" share a search for embodiment that migrates towards a "he" figure—whether this "he" is part of a disrupted love lyric with shades of the divine, or the "creature" who takes on his "earthly nature" to somehow slip into the figure of the beggar in the park. This beggar we might invoke as male, but I would suggest that here we might well hear Bishop remembering both the old woman in Stevens' *Owl's Clover*, layered with reference to Wordsworth's beggar who, in "Beggars" with her "tall Man's height," is encountered "pouring out sorrows like a sea;/Grief after grief," a "weed of glorious feature!" The female beggar is the ghostly, long-dead mother of two little boys, who becomes for Wordsworth the focus of a writer's block.[14] Bishop's interest in a poetry's musical ability to speak the "not-known" might best be exemplified in a letter to Marianne Moore on September 11, 1940, when she writes:

> I have that continuous uncomfortable feeling of "things" in the head, like icebergs or rocks or awkwardly placed pieces of furniture. It's as if all the nouns were there but the verbs were lacking—if you know what I mean. And I can't help having the theory that if they are joggled around hard enough and long enough some kind of electricity will occur, just by friction, that will arrange everything. But you remember how Mallarmé said that poetry was made of words, not ideas—and sometimes I'm terribly afraid I am approaching, or trying to approach it all, from the wrong track. (*OA* 94)

To suggest that Bishop was in any easy way, in her recall of music and the soporific songs of childhood, hankering for a place in which song and self met in a place of prelinguistic meaning that allied her to the losses of her early years, would do violence to the complexity of her work. "Little Exercise," "Late Air" and "Songs for a Colored Singer," the poems that immediately precede "Anaphora" as *North & South*, move towards its end, and which all carry a musical theme, all also employ anaphoristic repetition. In "Little Exercise," a poem masquerading as a musical study, there is no rhyme; instead the repetition through which we know the poem's scene creates a landscape around which someone sleeps "in the bottom of a row-boat/tied to a mangrove root or the pile of a bridge;/whom we must think of" (the only "think" which does not begin a sentence and which is not capitalized) "as uninjured, barely disturbed" (*PPL* 32). In "Songs for a Colored Singer" the lullaby sits like the song of the sirens between waking and sleeping, but also between life and death as the mother brings the child to a place of surrender both to her and itself: in which "Adult and child/sink to their rest./At sea the big ship sinks and dies,/lead in its breast" (*PPL* 38).

Lyric for Bishop comes to be seen not only as song that encompasses the social but as one which suggests a temporal model for the self that is less interested in a transcendental "ascent" than an embodied, relational structure where self emerges and imagines itself in a state of perpetual becoming. In a review headed "I Was But Just Awake," of Walter de La Mare's anthology for children, *Come Hither: A Collection of Rhymes and Poems of the Young of all Ages*, first reissued in 1958, Bishop writes about the relationship between voice and song and poetry:

At my house as I write there is a four-month-old baby who has just discovered his voice; not his crying voice, but his speaking, singing, or poetry-voice, and he devotes stretches of the day to trying it out. He can produce long trills, loud or soft, and repeated bird-like cries, obviously with pleasure. There is also a little black girl of three who vigorously pedals a tricycle around and around in a perfect time to an old Portuguese children's song. *Tere–sinha de Je–sus* she goes, in mixolydian (I think), telling another story about the same Teresa as Crashaw's (who is not in *this* book). And in the kitchen her mother sings one of this year's crops of sambas, "home-made" annually in endless variety by the poor Negroes of the slums, full of topical facts and preposterous fancies: *Come away with me on my little Lambretta,* she sings. (*PPL* 701)

There is much in this excerpt that offers a way in to Bishop's poetics. Here is voice, the child's cry elided with the cry of the bird; here is an antecedent in seventeenth-century verse, in nursery rhyme, in samba's seventeenth-century origins. Also, though, we hear Bishop's awareness of the poverty in which this music is made, of the communities and histories out of which song is made. Set alongside "Anaphora" we remember how music, those earlier evocations in the poem, is not, as we might expect, a weave of various sonorities to which an awakening self becomes aware. Instead a self is created through the rhythmic patterning of a poem, a model of movement, a process that allows for a momentary coalescence via an embodied self, the beggar—who is a material presence in and of the world, as well as a textual memory. As Bishop sits and writes, here again is past and present, improvization, and repetition, the baby boy's non-verbal cry, the rhythmic circling of the little girl on the bicycle whose rhythms sit in parallel with her mother's own domestic, composted song about a motorbike. There is also something deeply moving—an Elizabethan melancholy even—when we notice that this process, this emerging relationality, becomes known again in the contrapuntal energies between present and remembered mother, small baby and infant child.

NOTES

1. See manuscripts at Vassar College, Bishop 69.A1 Elizabeth Music; Bishop 71.3 Early Keyboard Music.
2. *Modernism and Music: An Anthology of Sources*, edited and with a commentary by Daniel Albright (Chicago and London: Chicago University Press, 2004) p. 27.
3. See *Hound &Horn* (July–September, 1934). See also *Hot Jazz and Jazz Dance* (Oxford: Oxford University Press, 1995).
4. See Gary Fountain, ed., *Remembering Elizabeth Bishop: An Oral Biography* (Massachusetts: University of Massachusetts Press, 1996).
5. Those visits also seem charged when set alongside the knowledge that Bishop never visited her mother during the 18 years she was committed to a mental hospital; the hospital's name here also surely creates a particular and resonant irony in the poem.
6. *Elizabeth Bishop: Life and the Memory of It* (Oakland: University of California Press, 1995) p. 81.
7. For a history of the Dolmetsch workshops, see https://www.dolmetsch.com/Dolworks.htm.

8. *Edgar Allan Poe and the Jukebox: Uncollected Poems, Drafts, and Fragments,* ed. and annotated by Alice Quinn (New York: Farrar Straus Giroux, 2006). See Gerard Manley Hopkins, "Sonnets of Desolation" or the "Terrible Sonnets," written between 1885 and 1886.

9. Wallace Stevens, *Collected Poems* (London: Faber, 2006).

10. Bishop had been travelling in Mexico with Marjorie where they had stayed for a while with Pablo Neruda. She goes on in that letter to add that the poem was finished in Key West. It is likely then that the poem, which was first published in *The Paris Review* in 1945, was finished between May 1945, when she received news that her first book was to be published by Houghton Mifflin and was asked to add more poems, and that autumn. Perhaps, with the bombing of Hiroshima and Nagasaki in early August 1945, even an awareness of the devastations of atomic energy is folded into the poem's resonances as well as its aesthetics. Certainly Bishop was anxious enough in thinking about the lack of references to the war in the book to ask that a note be made that most of the poems were written in 1942.

11. See Anne Stevenson, *Five Looks at Elizabeth Bishop* (Tarset: Bloodaxe, 2006) p. 92.

12. See Sarah Posman, "Modernist *Energeia*: Henri Bergson and the Romantic Idea of language" in Paul Ardoin, S.E. Gontaski, Laci Mattison, eds., *Understanding Bergson, Understanding Modernism.* (London: Bloomsbury, 2013) p. 219.

13. For an exploration of Bishop's later poetry, via Christopher Bollas" concept of the "unthought known," see my "Repetition and Poetic Process: Bishop's Nagging Thoughts" in Jonathan Ellis, ed., *Reading Elizabeth Bishop: An Edinburgh Companion* (Edinburgh: Edinburgh University Press, 2019) pp. 132–148.

14. See Wordsworth, *Selected Poems,* ed. Stephen Gill (London: Penguin) p. 131. Angus Cleghorn makes a convincing case for Bishop's engagement here with Wallace Stevens' old woman in "The Old Woman and the Statue" from *Owl's Clover,* "a figure excluded by the sculptor's transcendent vision" to whom Bishop directly refers in her letter to Marianne Moore when discussing her reading of Stevens. See "Bishop's Stevensian Architecture," unpublished conference paper. Elizabeth Bishop in Paris: Spaces of Translation and Translations of Space. University of Paris-Sorbonne, June 6–8, 2018. See also Thomas Frosch, "Wordsworth's "Beggars" and a brief instance of "Writer's Block" in *Studies in Romanticism,* vol. 21, no. 4, 1982, pp. 619–636.

CHAPTER 3

Music of the Sea: Elizabeth Bishop and Symbolist Poetics

Lisa Goldfarb

Abstract Elizabeth Bishop locates the mystery of the sea and its shore in many poems. The poem, however, which I return to is "At the Fishhouses," in which Bishop masterfully considers the juncture between the land and the sea. In "At the Fishhouses," she travels from the dense description of the land to the depths of the sea in three stanzas that call to mind sea poems in the French symbolist tradition. Bishop composes a music in "At the Fishhouses" that extends the works of Baudelaire, Rimbaud, and Valéry (and Stevens). This chapter unfolds in two parts: the first briefly places Bishop's poem in relation to the symbolist genre of sea poem, and the second comprises a close reading of "At the Fishhouses" in light of Valéryan theory.

This chapter is based on a longer version of my work on Bishop and the symbolists in Chapter V of my book, *Unexpected Affinities: Modern American Poetry and Symbolist Poetics*, published by Sussex Academic Press. I am grateful to the editor for acknowledging and agreeing to the publication of this current chapter.

L. Goldfarb (✉)
New York University, New York, NY, USA

A. Cleghorn (ed.), *Elizabeth Bishop and the Music of Literature*,
Palgrave Studies in Music and Literature,
https://doi.org/10.1007/978-3-030-33180-1_3

Keywords Poetics • Symbolist • Musicality • Resonance • Sea poems

I

In poem after poem, Bishop presents an evolving meditation on the sea and its environs: in "The Map," she questions the relation between land and sea when she asks, "is the land tugging at the sea from under?" (*PPL* 3); in "The Imaginary Iceberg," she addresses the sea as "floating field" and asks "are you aware an iceberg takes repose/with you, and when it wakes may pasture on your snows?" (*PPL* 4). In "Seascape," she has less to say about the sea, and more about everything that lies about it. In the second part of the poem, Bishop devotes her lines to a "skeletal lighthouse standing there/in black and white clerical dress" (*PPL* 31). I can point to more poems in which Bishop locates the mystery she finds in the sea and its shore ("The Sea and its Shore" is the title, too, of her 1937 story), for many titles come to mind: "The Sandpiper," "Song," "The End of March," and so poignantly, "Pleasure Seas," where "The water is a burning-glass/Turned to the sun" (*PPL* 223).

The poem, however, which I return to again and again is "At the Fishhouses," in which Bishop masterfully considers the juncture between the land and sea. In "At the Fishhouses," she travels the distance from the dense description of the land to the depths of the sea in three stanzas that call to mind, in remarkable ways, the genre of sea poems in the French symbolist tradition. Bishop composes a music in "At the Fishhouses" that seems to echo and extend the sea poems of Baudelaire, Mallarmé, Rimbaud, and Valéry (and even Stevens in the way he recalls the symbolists in "The Idea of Order at Key West").[1] This chapter will unfold in two parts: the first will briefly place Bishop's poem in relation to the symbolist genre of sea poem and turn very briefly to a few aspects of Valéry's musical poetics that we might apply to Bishop's poetic music; the second will comprise a reading of "At the Fishhouses" in light of Valéryan theory.

If the site of the sea as poetic subject unites Bishop to the French symbolists, her unusual "music" in "At the Fishhouses," with its three irregularly shaped stanzas describing the seascape in thick descriptive prose-like lines, seems to sharply separate her from the earlier poets. Baudelaire composes "Homme et la Mer," for example, in traditional French alexandrines in four stanzas of four lines each, which advance in a steady, consistent rhyme scheme. And Rimbaud's "L'Éternité," too, unfurls in a tightly rhythmic constructed form (six stanzas each of four lines in roughly five syllables), with identical first and last stanzas, opening and closing the poem with the lines that Bishop so admired in a heightened musical way: "*C'est la mer allée/Avec le soleil*" ("It is the sea gone off/With the sun" [Rimbaud, Fowlie 138, 139]).[2] Again, Bishop's seemingly casual and conversational sounding language at the beginning of "At the Fishhouses"— "Although it is a cold evening,/down by one of the fishhouses/ an old man sits netting" (*PPL* 50)—could not sound more distant from the highly rhythmic sounds of her French forebears.

Yet, as remote as Bishop's language might initially sound from the patterned conventional verse of the symbolists, it is crucial to bear in mind that at the same time the French symbolists (Baudelaire, Mallarmé, Rimbaud, and Valéry)[3] were composing verse in traditional French forms and that their work is also marked by a spirit of formal experimentation in their development of the prose poem and in their poetics, in which they work to articulate what constitutes musicality in verse—whether a poem is composed in tight verse form or descriptive prose. Bishop, it seems to me, composes "At the Fishhouses" in a music that recalls the rigorous attention to the sound of language in the symbolist sea poems, but in a way that innovates the form, both fulfilling the symbolist demand for Valéry's pendulum-like movement between sound and sense and stretching poetic form to include prose-like rhythms. There are essentially three ways that we might understand Bishop's "music" as fulfilling symbolist aims for poetic music. Let us briefly turn to Valéry, one of the poets working in the symbolist mode, who sets forth most clearly and comprehensively these essential components of musical poetry, and then to a reading of "At the Fishhouses" with Valéry's principles as our guide.

* * *

First, the music of lyric poetry, Valéry explains, resides in "*the indissolubilié du son et du sens*" [the indissolubility of sound and sense] (*Oeuvres I* 1333).[4] As a pendulum moves from one pole of language to the other in rhythmic fashion, so does the relationship between sound and sense (form and meaning) in lyric poetry.

> *Ainsi, entre la forme et le fond, entre the son et le sens, entre le poème et l'état de poésie, se manifeste une symétrie, une égalité d'importance, de valeur et de pouvoir qui n'est pas dans la prose. (Oeuvres I 1332)*

[Therefore, between form and meaning, between sound and sense, between the poem and the state of poetry there is a symmetry, an equal importance of value and power which is not the case in prose.]

Valéry asks us, then, to imagine the lyric poem as the ongoing and steady motion from one pole of language to the other—from sound to sense, and from sense or meaning back to form. Whether the poem is written in conventional form, free verse, or rhythmic prose, a condition for its identity as a lyric poem is this ongoing movement between sound and sense, form and meaning, the steady exchange between the concrete and abstract aspects of language.

However much we search for meaning in poetry, Valéry maintains, what distinguishes lyric poetry from prose is its characteristic voice, akin to music though not pure music. The second aspect of his poetic that we will apply to Bishop is his assertion that we cannot speak lyric poetry in the same way we use discursive language. Rather, the arrangement of the language, the form that the poet uses necessitates that we transform our voice when we read the poem. Valéry writes: "*Il faut et il suffit, pour qu'il y ait poésie certaine ... que le simple ajustement des mots, que nous allions lisant comme l'on parle, oblige notre voix, même intérieure, à se dégager du ton et de l'allure du discours ordinaire, et la place dans un tout autre mode et comme dans un tout autre* temps" [We know real poetry when the simple adjustment of words that we read in verse necessitates that we speak them, even to ourselves, in an entirely different way and as if in a completely different *time*] (*Oeuvres I* 450). While Valéry distinguishes between actual song and poetic song, he emphasizes that it is the musical dimension of lyric poetry that truly distinguishes it as poetry.

The third aspect of Valéry's musical poetic that strikingly applies to Bishop's unique music and her relation to the symbolists is his understanding of musical-poetic modulation. As a composer shifts keys in a musical piece, bringing the listener from one emotional register to another, so the poet in the lyric poem charts shifts in perception and feeling, as well as changes more manifest in the world about us. Musical-poetic modulation, Valéry writes, brings us from one "*manière de voir*" [manner of seeing] to another (M D V to M′ D′ V′, he writes in *Cahiers I* 629). The musical poet expresses "transformations" and uses modulation to transport the listener's soul from one state to another ("Images de la France" *Oeuvres II*, 1004).

II

"At the Fishhouses," at first, seems to defy association with music, so seemingly prose-like are its first few lines. Bishop's speaker opens the poem in an almost conversational tone and mood:

> Although it is a cold evening,
> down by one of the fishhouses
> an old man sits netting,
> his net, in the gloaming almost invisible,
> a dark purple-brown,
> and his shuttle worn and polished. (*PPL* 50)

The speaker begins with a prepositional phrase ("Although it is a cold evening") as if she were simply going to narrate a story—and she does indeed tell us a story with a time frame and physical setting that anchors us in time (evening) and space (at the fishhouses by the sea). The three stanzas present a narrative arc, in which the speaker walks and talks near the fishhouses and then by the sea. In the first stanza, we find the speaker "down by one of the fishhouses"; the speaker offers (using the first person) an old friend of her grandfather's a cigarette ("a Lucky Strike") and talks to him "of codfish and of herring" (*PPL* 51). In the second stanza, she walks to the water's edge, watches (or recalls watching) the activity there, where "they haul up the boats." And, in the third, she walks to the sea's edge, where she recalls many such evenings like this, especially her conversations with a particular seal ("One seal particularly") (*PPL* 51). The meticulous physical description, particularly of the first stanza, immerses the reader in the poem's setting.

Bishop binds us to the landscape in rich sensory images: we feel the chill of the air ("it is a cold evening"); we smell the strong "smells ... of codfish," and we see the "dark-purple brown" of the old man's "netting," the "steeply peaked roofs" of the fishhouses (*PPL* 50), and the silver sea along with fishermen's objects strewn about the landscape—benches, lobsterpots, masts, wheelbarrows, sea tubs, and more (*PPL* 50–51). It is as if Bishop were filling her lines with objects so as to keep us grounded in the very materiality she describes and in the physical world in which the speaker speaks to the friend of her grandfather. While it is in the first stanza that the speaker places us in the landscape, the descriptive detail continues in the second and third stanzas as well. In the second, as the speaker moves to "the water's edge," she shows us the "tree trunks ... laid horizontally" as they "haul up the boats" (*PPL* 51). In the third, Bishop reminds us of the cold and provides the feel of the "rounded gray and blue-gray stones" near and in the water and of the view of the trees, specifying that they are "dignified tall firs" (*PPL* 52) that surround the water.

One might legitimately ask how we might consider a poem that seems to be spoken in such prose-like tones with such realistic description of the land and seascape a musical poem in the Valéryan or symbolist sense. Yet, however much Bishop's poem tilts to one side of Valéry's pendulum at the beginning of the poem, it does not stay there long. While Bishop's conversational tones of "At the Fishhouses" that begin the poem and its narrative arc and rigorous physical description initially pull the poetic pendulum firmly toward the side of "meaning" or "sense," her use of the sonorous (and physical) aspects of language—specifically, word and phrase repetitions, consonance, and assonance—pull the reader back toward sound and the musical aspects of language in exactly the way that Valéry envisions. As we follow the speaker's voice in stanza 1, for example, for the story and setting, Bishop's repetitions urge us, as Valéry advocates the physical aspects of language do in lyric poetry, to dwell on the language in a way that consistently asks us to turn back to the language, to listen more closely, again and again. Just note the abundance of repetitions that creates a kind of doubling effect in the first stanza: "an old man sits netting,/ his net"; of the air "it makes one's nose run and one's eyes water"; "wheelbarrows" (two times); "iridescent" (two times); "codfish" (two times); "herring" (two times); "worn" (two times). The repetition of whole words and phrases is only one of the ways that Bishop composes the music of this verse. Together with the repetitions of words, her insistent consonance and assonance mark the lines and undercut the reader's expectation of easy resolution into meaning.

> All is silver: the heavy surface of the sea,
> swelling slowly as if considering spilling over,
> is opaque, but the silver of the benches,
> the lobster pots, and masts, scattered
> among the wild jagged rocks,
> is of an apparent translucence
> like the small old buildings with an emerald moss
> growing on their shoreward walls. (*PPL* 50–51)

When Bishop describes the surface of the sea, the sibilants and repetitive vowel sounds ("i" and "e") create an opaqueness (the language itself becomes physical!) in the language that Valéry identifies as the music of lyric poetry. Bishop thus gently turns, by way of repetition, consonance and assonance, a physical or realistic setting into a visionary one (the silver of sea and objects "is of an apparent translucence"). The repetitions of "silver" and the sibilants seem to erase the difference between land and sea, and Bishop seems to transform both. We first listen to the language to follow the narrative and to achieve a picture of the setting, and, before we are able to fix such a portrait, the repetitions pull us back to hear the language once again. Bishop composes "At the Fishhouses" so that in Valéryan terms she balances the relation between the *"sensation de la Voix"* [sensation of the voice] and *"fond"* [meaning] (*Oeuvres I* 1336), creating a rhythmic relation between the two.

For Valéry, as mentioned earlier, we know we are reading a poem when we cannot voice the poem as we would discursive prose, when we are reading either aloud or even silently to ourselves (*"même notre voix intérieur"*—even our interior voice). The form and arrangement of the poem forces us *"à se dégager du ton et de l'allure du discours ordinaire"* [to disengage from the tone and pace of ordinary discourse] (*Oeuvres I* 450) and to lift our voice to a kind of song (not pure song, but somewhere, he writes elsewhere, between voice and song).[5] While Bishop's untraditional structure in "At the Fishhouses" does not spur the kind of vocal shift that might characterize her more conventional rhythmic verse, as, for example, in "The Sandpiper," with its cadenced lines and the alternating rhymes that persist throughout, her packed descriptive lines in the poem, full of consonance and assonance in the first stanza alone, forbid recitation in a steady discursive voice. Her repetitions, too, and the sibilants that ring through the lines, surely signal that we speak the language in tones that grow increasingly charged as the poem continues.

The vocal transformation that Valéry identifies as the distinctive characteristic of the music of lyric poetry is especially evident in Bishop's third and last stanzas. Bishop continues to develop the narrative of the poem as the speaker faces the sea, and in a casual voice reminiscent of the conversational tones of stanza 1, she narrates her adventure with the seal, though this time the exchange between the speaker and the seal certainly signals to us that she describes, however incidentally, imaginative and even fantastic encounters. It is striking that in what many consider her prose-like poem, Bishop draws music into the very substance of the poem in the speaker's interaction with the seal. Poised at the sea's edge, she describes their interaction:

> Cold dark deep and absolutely clear,
> element bearable to no mortal,
> to fish and to seals ... One seal particularly
> I have seen here evening after evening.
> He was curious about me. He was interested in music.... (*PPL* 51)

But more important than the way she weaves music ("Baptist hymns" and "A Mighty Fortress is Our God" [*PPL* 51–52]) into the thematic texture of the poem is the way Bishop then counterpoints the narrative with the sonorous aspects of the poem (that is, the way she continues to balance sound and sense in the very fabric of the poem) that crescendo to its end. With the speaker's repetition of the first line—"Cold dark deep and absolutely clear"—to the end of the poem, Bishop's lines are sharply cadenced and full of repetitions and insistent vowel sounds and consonants that demand that the reader work, in Valéry's terms, to "*porter la voix au chant*" [to carry the voice to song] (*Oeuvres I* 667):

> I have seen it over and over, the same sea, the same,
> slightly, indifferently swinging above the stones,
> Icily free above the stones
> above the stones and then the world. (*PPL* 52)

It is hard to imagine a poem that fulfills more poignantly Valéry's description of the lyric poem as "*la voix en acte*" [the voice in action] (*Cahiers II* 1090). Bishop may begin with the conversational tones of the beginning ("Although it is a cold evening,/ down by one of the fishhouses"), but she modulates the voice so that by the poem's close we are at the sea's edge, at the very threshold of knowledge, not knowledge itself, but at its brink: "It is like what we imagine knowledge to be:/dark, salt, clear, moving, utterly free" (*PPL* 52).

Of all musical elements that he wishes to transpose into poetry, Valéry writes, "*L'idée de modulation comme je l'entends me ravit plus que toutes*" [The idea of modulation as I understand it captures me more than any other] (*Cahiers I* 297). One of the most striking aspects of "At the Fishhouses" is the way that Bishop "modulates" the poem, shifting the reader's point of view from one stanza to the next. As we have discussed, in the first stanza, Bishop anchors us in the landscape; in the second, she brings us "Down at the water's edge," and, in the third, to the "Cold dark deep" sea (*PPL* 51) Yet, Bishop brings the reader about and through the terrain, shifting changes in point of view within stanzas as well as from one to the next. We may be anchored in the landscape in the first half of stanza one, but then Bishop shifts our point of view from within the landscape: we are first among the "five fishhouses" and then amidst the "heavy surface of the sea,/swelling slowly" (*PPL* 50), and then our eyes move "Up on the little slope behind the houses." In stanza two, we are "down at the water's edge" and then "up the long ramp/descending into the water" where "tree trunks are laid horizontally" and then watch them go "down and down/at intervals at four or five feet." Finally, in the last stanza, we meet the "Cold dark deep" water with the speaker as she recounts what she has "seen here evening after evening." Bishop shifts our view of "one evening" to "evening after evening" (*PPL* 51), modulating from the particular evening to the continuous present: "I have seen it over and over." She then shifts our view from what the speaker has seen; that is from the continuous present, to the realm of the conditional—"If you should dip your hand in" and "If you tasted it" (*PPL* 52). Bishop's speaker then draws the reader close, addressing us in the second person, as she ushers us into the realm of metaphor: "It is like what we imagine knowledge to be …"

> drawn from the cold hard mouth
> of the world, derived from the rocky breasts
> forever, flowing and drawn, and since
> our knowledge is historical, flowing, and flown. (*PPL* 52)

Bishop, in the last lines of the poem, turns or modulates the lines so that we circle back to the beginning: the "rocky breasts" remind us of the landscape of the first stanza, and the water that is "flowing" (twice repeated) at the end of the poem echoes in sound the "gloaming" evening with which Bishop opens the poem and turns us back to the beginning to listen again.

When Valéry writes about the rhythmic movement between sound and sense that characterizes the music of lyric poetry, the vocal transformation at the heart of musical poetry, and his wish for lyric poems that shift keys as in music, it is hard to imagine that he could anticipate how Bishop in "At the Fishhouses" would achieve that rhythmic balance and modulation in such an innovative form and with such an unusual voice. Bishop's poem situates her speaker, and her reader along with her, firmly in the life of the land—"by one of the fishhouses" (*PPL* 50)—immersing us in dense descriptive detail, and then carries us from that detailed landscape into a fantastic visionary world at the water's edge—the "Cold dark deep and absolutely clear" (*PPL* 52) sea and the potential knowledge it brings. If Bishop does not create a pendulum-like movement from sound to sense with the steady rhythmic cadences of a conventionally structured poem like Baudelaire's "*L'Homme et la Mer*" ["Man and the Sea"] or Rimbaud's "*L'Éternité*," she achieves such balance between sound and sense otherwise. Her three stanzas unfold as musical movements might: in the 35 lines of the first, the speaker's conversational tones draw us in the landscape at the sea's edge; in the second movement, she transports us "down" from the land to the sea, as if on a bridge between the two, gently moving us from the rich sensory earth of the first stanza to the third, the longest and last movement, where we meet the sea in all its mystery. Valéry defines lyric poetry as "*le langage dont la forme, c'est à dire l'action et la sensation de la Voix, est de même puissance que le fond*" [the language in which the form, that is to say the action and sensation of the Voice, is of the same power as the meaning] (*Oeuvres I* 1336). Bishop may not compose "At the Fishhouses" in conventional poetic form, yet in the way the poetic speaker—the voice to which we listen—guides us from the "gloaming" sky of the first stanza to the "flowing" sea of the last and back again, she accomplishes a poem in which the "*sensation de la Voix*" [sensation of the voice] and "*le fond*" [meaning] are equally central to our understanding.

NOTES

1. See such poems as Baudelaire's "*L'Homme et la Mer*" ["Man and the Sea"], Mallarmé's "*Brise Marine*" ["Sea Breeze"] and "*Le Nénuphar blanc*" ["The White Water Lily"], Valéry's "*Le Cimetière marin*," and Rimbaud's "*L'Éternité.*"

2. Bishop writes in a letter to Anne Stevenson: "I've always thought one of the most extraordinary insights into the 'sea' is Rimbaud's *L'eternite*" (*PPL* 861).

3. Anna Balakian, in The Symbolist Movement: A Critical Appraisal, groups Baudelaire, Verlaine, and Mallarmé together as symbolists, and understands Valéry as working in the symbolist tradition. However, Balakian distinguishes Rimbaud from them. She writes, "What Rimbaud, Verlaine, and Mallarmé have in common is the fact that they produced their major works at the same time, in the early 1870's" (56). She goes further, "Rimbaud's

name belongs in the Symbolist ranks by personal association only." For the full discussion of her association of Rimbaud with the later surrealists rather than the symbolists, see *The Symbolist Movement*, Chapter IV (54–71). I group Rimbaud and Baudelaire together here for their mutual impact on Bishop, who did not see herself aligned with a particular school of poetry, but admired and drew from both late nineteenth-century French figures.

4. Translations from Valéry's prose are my own.

5. See Valéry's "Lettre à Madame C ...," in which he discusses his work with Croiza, an opera singer to bring poetry to a musical realm: "*je voulais essayer d'une voix qui descende ... de la mélodie pleine et entière des musiciens à la mélodie de poètes, qui est restreinte et tempérée*" [I wanted to try a voice which descends from a full musical melody to the melody of poets, which is more restrained and moderate] (*Oeuvres II* 1260). Valéry writes of the imprecise relationship of poetry and music throughout this essay as he details his work with Croiza (*Oeuvres II* 1260–1261).

CHAPTER 4

The Rhythm of Syntax in Elizabeth Bishop's "At the Fishhouses"

Yuki Tanaka

Abstract Since the publication of *North & South* in 1946, readers have often praised Elizabeth Bishop for her composure. Recent scholars have uncovered the troubled personal circumstances by reading her poetry autobiographically, which tends to overlook the linguistic resources Bishop uses to dramatize her description. One formal device that my chapter focuses on is syntax. "At the Fishhouses" begins with an objective description of a declining fishing town, but it becomes more personal halfway through, arriving at a visionary conclusion. Since this grand ending is uncharacteristic for Bishop, the second half of the poem has received more critical attention than the first. But an intense emotional drama is already underway from the beginning, and her syntax registers it quietly.

Keywords "At the Fishhouses" • Syntax • Rhythm • Perception

Since the publication of her first book *North & South* in 1946, readers have often praised Elizabeth Bishop for her composure. In his review of

Y. Tanaka (✉)
Hosei University, Tokyo, Japan

© The Author(s) 2019
A. Cleghorn (ed.), *Elizabeth Bishop and the Music of Literature*,
Palgrave Studies in Music and Literature,
https://doi.org/10.1007/978-3-030-33180-1_4

the book, Randall Jarrell notes that her "restraint, calm, and proportion are implicit in every detail of organization and workmanship" (*Elizabeth Bishop and Her Art* 180–181). Later scholars have tried to penetrate the calm surface of Bishop's description by reading her poetry autobiographically, mainly by using her unpublished material.[1] Bishop herself invites such autobiographical scrutiny when her "Giant Snail" says, "I give the impression of mysterious ease, but it is only with the greatest effort of my will that I can rise above the smallest stones and sticks" ("Rainy Season; Sub-Tropics," *PPL* 135). But critical accounts of her "workmanship" have been relatively few. As Bonnie Costello has pointed out, there is a frequent confusion in Bishop studies between biographical self and linguistically constructed speaker, resulting in "very little attention … not just to [a poem's] formal properties but its rhetorical ones, in creating the effect of an individual voice" (*American Literary History* 339).

My chapter focuses on how Bishop's language makes readers feel the emotional struggle with which her speaker observes, feels, and modifies her perceptions. One formal device Bishop uses to dramatize her description is syntax. We often talk about syntax in regard to experimental poetry; for example, it is hard to discuss language poetry without noting the use of fragmentary syntax.[2] Bishop's syntax looks more normative, but she occasionally displays her syntactic mastery, for example, by opening "The Moose" with a sentence that runs for 36 lines. Why, then, are we not talking about Bishop's syntax? One reason may be that we assume the natural ease of her voice so much that even when we do pay attention to her sentences, it is usually to demonstrate how she makes them sound colloquial. Eleanor Cook makes this assumption when she starts her brief discussion of Bishop's sentence structure by asking, "How do these sentences sound so right, so natural?" (119).

But sounding natural was never a big part of Bishop's own poetics. During her undergraduate years, she was deeply interested in the temporality of literature, which she called "rhythm," and wrote two essays on this subject. In "Time's Andromedas" (1933), Bishop ponders how novels create "a time-pattern of their own" in which events or paragraphs are read in relation to the previous ones and acquire new meaning. As opposed to the constant forward momentum of realist fiction (A happens, B happens), the kind of literature she is interested in creates "a sort of *experience-time*" (659). In "Dimensions for a Novel" (1934), Bishop fully explores her idea of rhythm by using T. S. Eliot's notion of the literary tradition in which the introduction of new work changes the reception of the previous work. Bishop argues that it is "equally true of the sequence of events or even of pages or paragraphs in a novel" (*PPL* 673). She is interested in "echoes and re-echoes, references and cross-references" (674), which require us to constantly adjust our understanding of past events or paragraphs; that is, these echoes demand "the complete absorption of each item, and the constant re-organization, the constantly maintained order of the whole mass" (679).

In Bishop's poems, such "constant re-organization" occurs on the level of rhythm, line by line, sentence by sentence, and dramatizes the changing perception of the speaker. For Bishop, rhythm was not just musical. It captures one's perception in flux, what she calls "a mind thinking." In a 1933 letter to Donald E. Stanford, she quotes a passage from "The Baroque Style in Prose" by M. W. Croll to describe "the sort of poetic convention I should like to make for myself":

> Their purpose (the writers of Baroque prose) was to portray, not a thought, but a mind thinking. … They knew that an idea separated from the act of experiencing it is not the idea that was experienced. The ardor of its conception in the mind is a necessary part of its truth. (qtd. in *One Art* 12)

Bishop's rhythm directs our attention to a mind at work. "At the Fishhouses" is a case in point. The poem begins with an objective description of a declining fishing town, but it becomes more personal halfway through, arriving at a visionary conclusion: "Since/our knowledge is historical, flowing and flown." Since this grand ending is uncharacteristic for Bishop, the second half of the poem has received more critical attention than the first. But an intense emotional drama is already underway from the beginning, and her syntax registers it quietly.

In the first half of "At the Fishhouses," Bishop's speaker tries to find beauty in the fishing town despite all evidence of decay. The poem starts with a typical Bishop sentence. The sentence is additive and hence feels spontaneous, as if the speaker observes and describes at the same time. The speaker does not voice her feeling, but we can tell from a series of images—the old man, his net made invisible by dusk, and his worn shuttle—that she is noticing the decline of the fishing town. Her observation feels unpremeditated as the main clause ("an old man sits netting") is modified by three noun phrases like afterthoughts ("his net," "a dark purple brown," and "his shuttle"). Moreover, Bishop places an adjective after a noun as in "the gloaming almost invisible" and "his shuttle worn and polished" to suggest that the speaker is observing these objects as she goes, just as we perceive an object and then think of its properties, not the other way around.

But soon her perception changes, and so does syntax. Hints of decay recede into the background, as if she was afraid of observing them too closely:

> The air smells so strong of codfish
> it makes one's nose run and one's eyes water. (*PPL* 50)

Despite the immediacy of this olfactory experience, we are not fully invited into the scene: the generic "one's," instead of the more intimate "you," creates distance between the scene and the reader. The scene becomes more and more distant as the poem proceeds:

> The five fishhouses have steeply peaked roofs
> and narrow, cleated gangplanks slant up
> to storerooms in the gables
> for the wheelbarrows to be pushed up and down on.

"One of the fishhouses" in the opening sentence becomes the less-specific "five fishhouses," and the singular "old man" becomes the plural "fishhouses" and "gangplanks." The speaker is zooming out, looking at these objects from such a distance that she can capture everything in a single glance. Accordingly, syntax becomes more constructed—this is not a spontaneous observation but a more premeditated one. Unlike the opening, additive sentence, which ends with a series of noun phrases, this sentence feels grammatically tighter as a group of prepositions bind each noun to its main clause: "slant *up to* storerooms *in* the gables/*for* the wheel barrows to be pushed *up* and *down on*." Bishop's speaker arranges the scene so carefully that the initial suggestion of decay is kept out of sight.

This vacillation between spontaneous syntax and premeditated syntax, between a close-up and a long shot, dramatizes "a mind thinking." The speaker observes the old man up close and backs away from this initial scene of decay, letting her mind drift over other parts of the town where she could find more beauty. As the poem starts to focus on the beauty of the town, Bishop's syntax becomes more composed to the point of creating neat symmetry. It is true that signs of decay are still present. The sea threatens to spill over and asserts its presence with sibilant alliteration ("...silver: the heavy surface of the sea,/swelling slowly as if considering spilling over"). But Bishop's syntax diminishes the sea's menacing presence: its swelling is bracketed by the subject ("the heavy surface of the sea") and the predicate ("is opaque"). Similarly, Bishop inserts another image of disorder—"scattered/among the wild jagged rocks"—between "the silver" and "is of an apparent translucence." She repeats the syntactic pattern of the first clause (subject-participle-simile-predicate) in the next clause, except that the simile is pushed to the very end of the second clause:

<first clause>	<second clause>
the heavy surface of the sea	but the silver of the beaches …
swelling slowly	scattered among the wild jagged rocks
as if considering spilling over	
is opaque	is of an apparent translucence
	like the small old buildings.

(50–51)

The closing simile does not conform to this otherwise perfect parallelism, which mirrors the speaker's conflicted attitude toward the sea. She notes that the sea is a source of beauty ("silver," "emerald," "translucence"), but that the beauty of fish scales is illusory ("*apparent* translucence") and the sea can be an agent of destruction as the moss encroaches on the "small old buildings." "Old" recalls "old man," bringing back the speaker's initial observation of the declining town.

In the next sentence, this ambivalence about the town's decay is resolved for a moment. Earlier in the poem, the wheelbarrows are "pushed up and down" as tools for routine labor. Now both the wheelbarrows and the tubs are covered with iridescent fish scales. Syntactic symmetry is nearly perfect, emphasizing the town's beauty with the architectural beauty of sentence structure:

<first clause>	<second clause>
The big fish tubs	and the wheelbarrows
are completely lined	are similarly plastered
with layers of beautiful herring scales	with creamy iridescent coats of mail
	with small iridescent flies crawling on them.

(51)

The rhyme of "scales" and "mail" calls attention to an elaborate syntactic chiasmus where "layer" chimes with "mail," and the three-word phrase "beautiful herring scales" with "creamy iridescent coats." "With creamy iridescent coats of mail" also echoes "with small iridescent flies." Unlike the less-balanced parallelism of the previous sentence, this Latinate, symmetrical sentence dispels any presence of decay that has haunted the poem up to this point.

By now, Bishop has established a relationship between syntax and perception. The poem has moved away from the additive construction of the opening sentence to more premeditated, symmetrical sentences; accordingly, the presence of decay has been diminished in favor of iridescent beauty. In "Dimensions for a Novel" Bishop describes "echoes and re-echoes" and the constant readjustment of a pattern that each new element requires of readers. In the same way, Bishop sets up a correspondence between the town's beauty and symmetrical syntax, only to subvert it and indicate a change in the speaker's perception. In the next sentence the poem continues the parallelism of the previous sentence as if to prolong a moment of iridescent beauty: "**Up** on the little slope behind the houses,/ set in the sparse bright sprinkle of grass" (51). These two lines are metrically similar, the first line being a variation of an iambic pentameter and the second a tetrameter, both starting with a trochaic substitution. The lines also share vowels and consonants in "little"/"sprinkle," "behind"/"bright," and "slope"/"sparse." However, this light, iambic, parallel rhythm is disrupted in the next lines, where Bishop sounds a darker note:

> Up on the little slope behind the houses,
> set in the sparse bright sprinkle of grass
> is an ancient wooden capstan,
> cracked, with two long bleached handles
> and some melancholy stains, like dried blood,
> where the ironwork has rusted. (51)

"Is an ancient wooden capstan" has the same iambic lilt, but is quickly interrupted across the line-ending by the word "cracked."

"Cracked" is jarring in several ways. Not only does it reintroduce the theme of the town's decay, it also comes right after "capstan," which sounds phonetically close to "cracked" and hence calls attention to itself. Moreover, "cracked" introduces the first internal punctuation in a long time—the last ones we saw are back in lines 15–16 ("is opaque, but the silver of the benches,/the lobster pots, and masts, scattered"). With no internal interruption, the poem has been reading smoothly up to this point, so the comma after "cracked" creates a strong, unexpected caesura, especially across the line-ending. A change in rhythm signals a change in perception. "Cracked" leads to further evidence of decay ("two long bleached handles," "some melancholy stains"). By noting the cracked capstan, the speaker announces her determination to see the world more clearly, however uncomfortable this perception may feel. Frank Bidart once said, "I'm scared to imagine *observing* as much as Miss Bishop does" (*Elizabeth Bishop and Her Art* 214). Bishop's gaze here is uncompromising: she clarifies "some melancholy stains" by comparing it to the more visual "dried blood," and then by literalizing it as "rusted." At the end of the sentence, all appearance of iridescent beauty, all figurative embellishment, has been stripped away.

Such a rhythmic and perceptual shift happens most explicitly in the transitional second verse paragraph. Having observed the presence of decay on land, the speaker now looks toward the sea, which she has implicitly described as a source of both beauty and decay. The strophe is peppered with prepositions, which orient us spatially: "Down at the water's edge, at the place/where they haul up the boats, up the long ramp/descending into the water" (*PPL* 51). The last line of the strophe—"at intervals of four or five feet"—is exact, rather fussy, providing a specific measurement of how far the trucks are from each other. In addition to spatial order, the line also suggests metrical order. Susan Stewart argues that "intervals of four or five feet" is a "self-referential pun" on the way the poem has been wavering between tetrameter and pentameter (*Poetry and the Fate of the Senses* 140). But this spatial and metrical arrangement is upset across a stanza break, as soon as the speaker comes into contact with the sea:

Cold dark deep and absolutely clear,
element bearable to no mortal,
to fish and to seals...

The iambic cadence of "four or five feet" is replaced by a series of stressed monosyllables: "Cold dark deep." Moreover, Bishop's grammatical, exact sentence dissolves into an incomplete sentence that consists entirely of adjectives ("Cold dark deep ... clear"), an adverb ("absolutely"), and abstract words ("element," "bearable," "mortal"). Syntactic fragmentation represents a kind of deadlock: the speaker cannot use her descriptive language to capture the sea.

Now Bishop's speaker changes her tack, approaching the sea not through objective description but by foregrounding personal memory. From this point on, her syntax turns from rigorous and symmetrical to more colloquial. There has been an instance of colloquial syntax earlier in the poem, but it has never been dominant. For example, after confronting the cracked capstan and the rusted ironwork, the speaker reintroduces the old man in two short simple sentences: "The old man accepts a Lucky Strike./He was a friend of my grandfather" (*PPL* 51). Bishop foregrounds this earlier colloquial note immediately after the fragmentary second verse paragraph: "One seal particularly/I have seen here evening after evening." The first appearance of "I" makes the poem more colloquial, and repetition adds a casual, spontaneous tone ("evening after evening," "He was …. He was" "about me … like me"). The poem becomes so colloquial that Bishop even uses a cliché to describe the seal emerging from the sea with a shrug "as if it were against his better judgment" (52). The syntax of the poem becomes looser and more repetitive: "Then he would disappear, then suddenly emerge," "Cold dark deep and absolutely clear,/the clear gray icy water," "a million Christmas trees stand/waiting for Christmas." This tonal change is most explicit when the earlier stiff phrase "of an apparent translucence" relaxes into more colloquial diction: "The water *seems* suspended/above the rounded gray and blue-gray stones" (52, my emphasis).

This loosening of syntax signals a change in the speaker's attitude toward the sea. She cannot describe the sea with visual exactitude, so she gradually transports it from the physical world to the imaginative world, where its destructive nature can be fully fathomed. Earlier in the poem, repetition is used to clarify or modify initial perceptions; for example, the speaker elaborates on the image of the old man "netting" by adding, "his net, in the gloaming almost invisible." But here, repetition is used not for visual clarification but to propel the poem with the sheer force of music. The lines speed up, carried by iambs and anapests (e.g. "I have seen it over and over"), tripping lightly across the page. This cadence launches the poem from the minute physical reality of "stones" to the vaguer "world," to the imaginative world of "if": "If you should dip your hand in" (52). Bishop also uses the word "transmutation," which attests to the alchemical imagination of a poet who transforms water into fire, into a vision. Infusing the physical world with the imagination, the speaker can finally confront the sea as an agent of destruction ("ache," "burn," "feeds"). The first appearance of the second-person pronoun also indicates this psychological development: earlier she used "one's" ("makes one's nose run and one's eyes water") to distance the scene of decay, but here she makes the sea more immediate by exposing "you" to its erosive force. Instead of "swinging above the stones," the sea erodes both the living ("hand") and the inanimate ("stones"). Bishop emphasizes this apocalyptic vision by varying metrical rhythm: "Your bones would begin to ache and your hand would burn" is an iambic pentameter with anapests in the second and fourth feet, and while the last line imitates this smooth, iambic lilt, a string of stressed monosyllables "dark gray flame" troubles it and underlines the sea's fiery violence.

The speaker seems to have arrived at an all-encompassing vision about the mortality of the human world and the destructive force of the sea. But the rhythm of the closing lines agitates this visionary note, challenging even a glimmer of epistemological certainty as well as the speaker's agency. The sea is so elusive that it does not correspond exactly to knowledge but "what we imagine knowledge to be." Symmetrical syntax returns, this time not to suggest a sense of order or aesthetic control, but to reflect the sea's intractability. Here, syntactic parallelism ("If you should dip. ... If you tasted it," "drawn from ... derived from," "flowing and drawn ... flowing and flown") feels more agitated as the sentence stops and starts, heavily punctuated and drawn across line-endings for strong enjambment. Moreover, although the final sentence sounds well-structured, almost syllogistic—if A, if B, then C—and seems to impose grammatical order on the sea, it does not lead to the kind of epistemological comfort the syntax promises. "Flowing and flown" seems to repeat the pattern of "drawing and drawn," describing the ebb and flow of the ocean, but "flown" is the past participle of "fly," which makes knowledge fly away out of human reach. The poem ends with this feeling of uncertainty over what the speaker has come to know as a result of her intense observation. The final lines suggest that any knowledge is outside her grasp, and the troubled rhythm of the final sentence seems to yield her agency over to the fluctuation of the sea and its elusiveness.

Syntax works upon our minds in a subtler way than imagery or diction. It is about the order in which details are parceled out to readers. Like music, these details create a pattern that gets altered as we move down the lines. We do not normally think of such sequencing and patterning because we take it for granted, but it is crucial to the way we respond to a poem. In "Rhythm as Coping," Alexander Freer emphasizes rhythm as relational, as the reader's way of "coping" or grappling with a text. When we read a poem, line by line, word by word, we are not sure what comes next, but we cope with this uncertainty by using our knowledge of what has come before, trying to create a pattern, and being surprised when the next word subverts it. Freer emphasizes this experiential aspect of reading poetry by proposing "a concept of rhythm that begins with our perceptions of surprise in the face of predictability and order in the face of disorder" (560). Once we start paying attention to the way we read experientially and respond to the slight modulation of rhythm, "At the Fishhouses" becomes more dynamic than it seems. The first half of the poem does not generally attract as much attention as its grand, visionary ending, because the initial emotional drama feels understated. But by tracing the rhythm of the poem, we can highlight the speaker's vacillation between beauty and decay as well as her gradual acknowledgment of the sea as violent and unfathomable. In a sense, syntax is a perfect device for reticent poets like Bishop: she does not have to spell out any of these shifting emotions, but instead she choreographs her sentences so quietly that they move us without our knowing.

NOTES

1. For a critique of autobiographical reading in Bishop studies, see Langdon Hammer, "The New Elizabeth Bishop," *Yale Review* 82:1 (1994): 135–149, and Bonnie Costello, "Elizabeth Bishop's Impersonal Personal," *American Literary History* 15.2 (2003): 334–366.
2. See Bob Perelman, *The Marginalization of Poetry* (Princeton University Press 1996): 59–78. Perelman argues that language poets use syntactic fragmentation to expose the lyric voice as written, as a linguistic construct.

CHAPTER 5

"Hearing Things": Voice and Rhyme in the Poems of Elizabeth Bishop

Andrew Eastman

Abstract This chapter addresses voice in Bishop's poems by looking at how the poems function as encounters with other voices and sounds in which the speaker's own voice is echoed back to her. Through such encounters, subjectivity in the poem, the way the poem makes a place for the reader's voice, for indefinite re-enunciation, is at stake, most specifically because the voices of others are sounded through the poem's network of signifiers. An examination of speechsound patterning in "Large Bad Picture," "Twelfth Morning; or What You Will," and "The Monument" shows that the way things look, feel, and sound in Bishop's poems is inseparable from their networks of phonemic patterning; by sounding other voices the poem makes a place for the reader's voice to emerge.

Keywords Bishop • Voice • Rhyme • Sound • Speech

A. Eastman (✉)
University of Strasbourg, Strasbourg, France

© The Author(s) 2019
A. Cleghorn (ed.), *Elizabeth Bishop and the Music of Literature*,
Palgrave Studies in Music and Literature,
https://doi.org/10.1007/978-3-030-33180-1_5

41

"Voice," it could be argued, is a key element of the "music" of poems: and voice in Elizabeth Bishop's poems is the speaker's voice, the quality of speech in the written medium, the voice *of* the poem, the poem's use of syntax, rhythm, intonation, inflection to create the impression of a mind thinking, the sound of the "natural" speaking voice, "natural tone" (Cook 8), "dark music coupled with a deceptive vernacular" (Boland), "the illusion of utter transparency," as the title of a recent article in *The New York Review of Books* phrased it (Galassi 26). Bishop herself claimed that what distinguished Brazilian poetry from Anglo-American was that the Brazilians "don't write the way they speak" (Brown 290). Yet the speaker's voice is, of course, not the only voice in Bishop's poems—witness the "oh" of Aunt Consuelo: the poems make a place for other voices and for a wealth of aural phenomena. The power of Bishop's poems derives from their openness to what is "out there," and what is "out there" is not only the visible texture of reality but also things heard, sound and voice. Another approach to the speaking voice in Bishop's poems might see it, then, as a way of attesting, absorbing and echoing other voices, other sounds, sounds and voices located ambiguously inside and outside the speaker, and which echo her own voice back to her.[1]

Voice in Bishop's poems would then be also what estranges voice or compels attention to the strangeness of the words with which one attempts to render sound, the strangeness of speechsound *as* sound. If Bishop's poems are attached to places, to the description of places and things seen, it often seems that what is seen there is inseparable from what is heard there, or that seeing is complicated by the sense of hearing. Place in Bishop's poems is, often, the "scene" of an encounter with voice, or with an analogue of voice; with voice as language, or with sound as a kind of proto-voice, voice outside of language: the hermit's voice and its echo in "Chemin de Fer"; the rain's echolalia and the mother's voice, "ugly as sin," in "Squatter's Children"; the "Click. Click." of the dredge in "The Bight"—voices whose relation to the speaker's remains indeterminate. Here the prototype is Bishop's story "In the Village": the scream is "in" the landscape, in the color of the sky; what is at stake then is how the scream comes to inhabit the story or poem, to live in its words. If the scene in some of Bishop's work is a setting for the emergence of a sound or voice, then what is at stake is the way this sound or voice is written into the poem.

Perhaps this encounter with voice or sound that animates some of Bishop's poems could be read through the conception of voice presented by Mladen Dolar in his book *A Voice and Nothing More*. Dolar approaches the voice from a Lacanian perspective; he argues that voice is characterized by what Lacan called "extimacy" (96), that is to say located both inside and outside the body, both inside and outside language. This might be a fruitful approach to the way sound and voice are encountered and brought into Bishop's poems. Dolar's conception of the voice makes a place for the analyst, whose silence echoes the patient's voice back to him, and is thus "the embodiment [...] of the voice" and "pure enunciation" (124); in response to this silence, writes Dolar, "our fate as linguistic, ethical, political subjects has to be pulled to pieces and reassembled" (124). Such a "fate" then would not, apparently, concern the *poetic* subject—the "voice" of the poem so to speak—which comes into its own as the *reader's* co-enunciation of the text, the reader's activity in the text. And though Mladen Dolar includes chapters on the "metaphysics," the "physics," the "ethics" and the "politics" of the voice, his account includes no chapter on the "poetics" of the voice. This suggests that voice in poems must be seen otherwise: that what is at stake in the voices of Bishop's poems is how the speaker's voice comes into its own as the "echo" of another voice—*and*, how the speaker's voice makes a place, as *poetic* subject, for the reader's voice to come into its own.

How does it? I will try to argue here that sound and voice as encountered in Bishop's poems are echoed into the poem, and subjectified, through rhyme, by which I mean not only end rhyme and canonical rhyme, but the whole network of speechsound repetitions associating signifiers in a poem and collection of poems; "music," then, in the sense in which T. S. Eliot speaks, in "The Music of Poetry," of "the music of a word" as "aris[ing] first from its relation to the words immediately preceding and following it, and indefinitely to the rest of its context" (32), the "music of poetry" being "not something which exists apart from the meaning" (29). Rhyme is clearly an essential component of poems for Bishop: Alice Quinn notes the "lists and lists of end rhyme words" in Bishop's notebooks (Bishop *Edgar Allan Poe* 273),[2] which suggests that she might have endorsed Baudelaire's remark that "any poet, who doesn't know exactly how many rhymes each word has, is incapable of expressing any idea whatsoever" (183).[3] Aural experience, our experience of what "sounds" outside of us, is brought into the poem, we say, by means of imitation, sound symbolism. Thus T. V. F. Brogan, in his article on "sound" in the *New Princeton Encyclopedia of Poetry and Poetics*, noted a preponderance of "sibilants" in the beginning of Robert Frost's poem

"Desert Places" and explained it by claiming that sibilants "are the sounds that snow makes" (1174). Yet Bishop's poems do not simply mobilize supposed inherent qualities of English phonemes; they *invent* ways of suggesting correspondences between phonemes and auditory phenomena. Such inventions work *through* the networks of phonemic echoes in the poem. Imitation in this sense does not give access to the sounds of the world; it makes language stranger, voice more opaque; it makes for excess in language. Voice, then, can no longer be transparent. In Bishop's poems imitative invention intersects with the purely linguistic network of signifiers through which like-sounding words motivate each other; voice is diffused throughout the poem. I propose then to look at several poems where encounters with sound or voice involve the speaker's encounter with her own voice: "Large Bad Picture," "Twelfth Morning; or What You Will," and "The Monument."

"Large Bad Picture" (*PPL* 8–9) is a good illustration of the way voice emerges from landscape in Bishop's poems. The poem is not a description of a place, but of a painting of a place; the description of the place in the painting prepares the emergence of sound in stanzas five and six:

> And high above them, over the tall cliffs'
> semi-translucent ranks,
> are scribbled hundreds of fine black birds
> hanging in *n*'s in banks.
>
> One can hear their crying, crying,
> the only sound there is
> except for occasional sighing
> as a large aquatic animal breathes. (*PPL* 9)

Here sound is, curiously, a form of writing, which exemplifies the "badness" of the picture: the artist's birds don't look like birds but rather like scribbled letter "*n*'s," crude forms of visual representation. The world of the painting is one where writing or inscription is encountered in nature, as in book six of Wordsworth's *Prelude*—but here, not as the visible vestige of God's creative act but as inept art. These "*n*'s" are marked in Bishop's text by italics and thus carefully distinguished from the poem itself, carried over from the painting into the poem. But the written letter is also, inseparably, the phoneme/n/, as soon as we read the "*n*'s" or birds; the birds are letters *and* phonemes. This is presumably why we "hear" the sounds they make in the next line: precisely at the moment when the artifice of representation has been seen through, it seems the viewer is absorbed into the imaginary world of the picture, where the birds' "crying, crying" becomes audible.

The emergence of this sound in the "space" of the poem has the effect of "thickening" the poem's language. Bishop multiplies "*n*'s" in the line "hanging in *n*'s in banks," where the letter appears six times: two occurrences of the phoneme /n/ in the repeated preposition "in" framing the written letter "*n*" are in turn framed by three occurrences of the related nasal /ŋ/ in the words "hanging" and "banks," as though the carryover of the symbol from painting to page had the effect of charging and slowing the awkward syntax of the line. Here the parallel construction "in *n*'s in banks" uncannily confuses the painting's surface and its represented space, in phrasing decidedly not "natural." These phonemes echo into the following stanza, where final /n/ appears in "One" standing for the speaker and "can," while /ng/ is repeated in "crying, crying." It becomes apparent, then, that these "*n*'s" are part of a larger network: "ranks," "banks" and "crying" all echo "great-uncle," the relational term applied to the artist; while the sequence of letters *n-s* and the sequence of phonemes /nz/ which we find in "*n*'s" make an internal rhyme of sorts with "semitranslucent" in which the morpheme "trans-" evokes the traversing of representational boundaries which the scribbled letter's appearance in the poem seems to effect. The same pair of letters ("n"-"s") recurs further in a sequence of words at the poem's end, including "sound," "sun," "sunset," "consoling" and "consider." By calling our attention to the morphemic construction of these last two words, which we divide, etymologically, at the junction between "n" and "s" ("con-sole," "con-sider"; also "contemplation"), punning meanwhile on the sun in "console," the poem seems to lay bare, as "fine-sounding" amalgamations of letters, the Latinate terms we traditionally bring forth to dignify aesthetic appreciation.

The emergence of sound into the text thus seems to coincide with the emergence of the speaker and viewer herself. It is the speaker, we suppose, who "reads" "*n*'s" into the painting and then hears the "crying" and "sighing" of animals; the way these sounds are introduced also manifests her presence. Thus the rhyme or consonance linking "is" and "breathes" in the above-quoted passage seems intended to imitate the "sighing" of the "large aquatic animal," particularly by sounding the fricatives /z/ and /ð/; the voiced fricative in end position has the effect of lengthening the vowel of a stressed monosyllable, and the rhyme accentuates this effect, extending "breathes" into a sigh. This sighing rhyme is made audible on the one hand by meter and phrasing, for the line contrasts the long noun-phrase tone group "a large aquatic animal" with the monosyllabic tone group "breathes," which concludes the stanza; and likewise through the /z/ inflection of present tense, of "actualization" in the present, by means of which "being" and "breathing" are identified. This "breathing" would seem to be a "breaching" of the poem's pictorial surface, by which the viewer's—or reader's—own "breathing" is made audible within the picture and within the poem. The voice which appears in the landscape would then seem to coincide with the speaker's or reader's own voice, refracted through the media of painting and poem, where it surfaces as rhyme.

In "Twelfth Morning, or What You Will" (*PPL* 89–90), the emergence of sound or voice in the landscape is similarly a way of gauging, or negotiating, the speaker's place in it, here again connected to the sounding of breath. Set in "Cabo Frio," a seaside town where Bishop spent several Christmas holidays, the poem is the second-to-last in the "Brazil" section of *Questions of Travel*; it presents a world in which ordinary exploitation and hopelessness, the "Company's" depredations, the brokenness of things questions the viewer's or speaker's place in it, where her "perspective" may not go unquestioned. The landscape is then framed or distanced through the evocation of epiphany and its traditions of masquerade and inversion: "things" perform through their personifications, while the speaker's "I" is masked by the "you" of Shakespeare's title and deflected onto the quoted speeches of can and boy. The meanings of the visual scene emerge, along with the speaker's sense of self, in what is heard. Describing place, in stanza three, is an occasion for "dreaming audibly" (*PPL* 48):

> The sea's off somewhere, doing nothing. Listen.
> An expelled breath. And faint, faint, faint
> (or are you hearing things), the sandpipers'
>   heart-broken cries. (*PPL* 89)

Here aural phenomena are explicitly associated with auditory hallucination, with "hearing things": they are thus made equivalent with hearing *oneself*. The word "Listen," and the several full stops marking pauses, compel attention to speechsound. Evoking breath, Bishop works again with the repetition of voiceless fricatives, which depend, of course, on the emission of breath without voice: /s/, in "sea's," "something," "Listen," "expelled" and "sandpipers'"; /θ/ in "nothing," "breath," "things"; /f/ in "off" and "faint, faint, faint"—speechsounds which bring breathing into the poem ("expelled breath" thus condenses the title word "Twelfth"). Meanwhile, the repetition in "faint, faint, faint" is Bishop's invention of a way of suggesting auditory experience: the repetition enacts the sound of the repeated cries in the poem; or alternatively, their reverberation and progressive fading in the mind, a sound *growing* fainter and fainter. How does one *read* "faint, faint, faint"? One is led to *perform* the aural quality of the sounds, in a manner, again, not obviously natural; with "faint" here working as what David Nowell Smith calls a "figuration" of voice (12), making voice itself audible.

Listening thus seems to make a place for the speaker—and reader—in the scene. But voice is not only figure, rhetoric; it is the poem's speech-sound continuum. The words which designate sounds are written into the poem's system of rhymes and phonemic echoes. The presentation of the scene comes to a close with the song of Balthazár; otherwise stated, the phrase "hearing things" lays a framework in which the poem's festive context may achieve a climax through singing: "things" is the only word ending in /iŋz/ before the final stanza and so prepares the concluding rhyme of "sings" with "Kings," the poem's only canonical end rhyme. The focus on "breath" and "hearing things" prepares the reintroduction of the name "Balthazár" which contains the consonantal sequences /b-θ/ and /θ-z/, connecting, thus, the singing boy with the speaker-reader. Words which denote sound in "Twelfth Morning" thus mark the speaker's and reader's presence in the poem and connect them to the singer, while the rhyme linking "hearing things" and "sings" points implicitly to the reader's role in sounding the poem's rhymes. The poem's music is thus caught up in a fragile, provisional, recursive practice of "hearing things," the hearing of a precarious, incipient self, inscribed at the threshold of perception.

"Twelfth Morning," with its panoply of performing persons, house, fence, horse, can and boy, could be read as a revisiting of Hopkins's poem "As Kingfishers Catch Fire"; the connection is suggested by the way "everything" and "things" are echoed by the present participle forms "sticking," "doing," "hearing," "dozing," "approaching," "flashing," "slap-slapping" and "singing." But whereas Hopkins describes a world in which all things "deal out" their essences, in which each thing "selves," "Twelfth Morning" enacts self through the opacity of foreignness, through the otherness of the poem's aural and visual phenomena and the way they are phrased. Thus, for example, in Balthazár's song, Bishop, perhaps also for prosodic reasons, has used not "birthday" but "anniversary," seemingly a calque of Portuguese "aniversário," just as "Day of Kings," which does not seem to be an English phrase, adapts the Portuguese "Dia de Reis." The song then escapes our linguistic expectations, creating a context in which the image of the "black boy" can be displaced, in which boy and speaker may be identified: "Balthazár," with stressed final /är/, more closely echoes the stressed syllable of "heart-broken," the word which encompasses what the poem's "you" hears. "Personality" might then be understood in terms of what sounds through a foreign medium, just as the poem's objects "show through" the mist; "personality" and "perspective" are here conjoined and inseparable.

The poem's representation of subjectivity, its incipient "you," is then a function of its networks of speechsound. The sequence *per(s)-/*pər(s)/, which we find in "personality" and "perspective," echoes through a series of associated terms: "perhaps," "sandpipers," the fence's "pure rust," "pewter-colored," "pearl," as well as, marginally, in "shopworn" and "shipwreck," both of which connect through their written sequence *pw(-)r* to "pure" and "pewter-colored." How might we read this series of words? "Pure" and "pewter-colored" are the only signifiers in the poem which contain, like "you," initial /j/.[4] The first is ironized though its inclusion in the construction "pure rust," which associates purity and corruption; while "pewter" designates one of many metallic substances referred to in Bishop's work, related, notably, to qualities of paint—as for example "titanium white" in "Poem," (*PPL* 165)—here, glossed by the phrase "ancient mixture," which likewise echoes "pure," "pewter" qualifies the color of the horse, originally said to be "white"—adding another color to the palette, which up to this point contains only "white," the specifically racial "black," and their composite, "gray"; suggesting, thus, how the horse's color changes as we look at it; and in that it echoes the poem's "you" (/pju-tər/), how both seer and seen are caught up in and emerge from the process of hearing, and voicing, things.[5]

This sense of self and voice as processual, emerging in other, heard voices, carries over to the sphere of art. If the seen world is, relatively, static, sound or voice emerging into the poem brings the poem into time, grounds the poem's temporality and implies by the same token a temporality of art. If the work of art in Bishop's practice of art must be in some way achieved, brought to perfection, this is only insofar as it is also capable of beginning again, only insofar as it authorizes rebeginning and rereading. The monument in "The Monument" (*PPL* 18–20) is "the beginning of a painting." The monument of this poem is seen, not heard: "Why does that strange sea make no sound?" says the viewer. Yet, at the same time, the monument seems to emerge into sound, for, some lines further on, "the monument is cracking." "Cracking" denotes a process which may be seen, or inferred from visible signs, if we think of paint flaking or wood fissuring; but also, theoretically, heard, for "cracking" is of course sound. In the case of "The Monument," however, we assume the process is too slow, too prolonged, for the sound to be perceived; this "cracking" of the monument is, again, imaginary sound—"hearing things."

Yet it is this cracking which makes possible and ushers into the poem another way of seeing the monument, as a "thing" caught up in time. Whereas the monument was first "cracked," the subsequent use of present tense with progressive aspect in "is cracking" predicates process; and the verb phrase works as the poem's turning point, at once closing the series of quoted complaints expressed by an impatient viewer and introducing the idea that the monument is "alive" partakes of life to the extent that it is caught up in change, or, as Walter Benjamin suggested in "The Translator's Task," to the extent that it has a history.[6] The verbal phrase "is cracking" is followed in the poem by a series of -ing participles, "looking," "having life," "wishing," "wanting"; and the proliferation of -ing forms in this part of the text is brought to a climax with the line "It is the beginning of a painting," where the two nouns in -ing ("beginning," "painting") suggest that the process has been brought into the object. Meanwhile, the "sound" of "cracking," we might say, is projected through a series of like-sounding words, which include "crates," "cramped," "crated scenery," "decorations," "carelessly," "crudest scroll-work" and "commemorate," a network of signifiers which combines artifice and nature (not unlike the series of frottages Max Ernst published under the title Histoire naturelle in 1926, which Bishop particularly appreciated), the "crated" and the "crude," and points, through the collocation of "cracking" and "decorations," both construed as signs of life in the monument, to the simultaneously destructive and creative forces at work in art, the capacity of a work to reinvent itself.

The monument, then, is a soundscape. By bringing the representation of sound and voice into the words of the poem, Bishop explores a dialectic of voice, which, according to Dolar, is simultaneously and indeterminately inside and outside the body, like breath: sounds and voices perceived are echoes, versions of our voices, in turn voiced in the echoes of rhyme. In Dolar's account of the indeterminate location of voice, it exceeds the signifier, such that "there is no linguistics of the voice" (19). But poetic voice must be looked for in-between signifiers, in the space where reading signifies. The beginning of a poem, we might then argue, is when the voice "cracks," when its own "naturalness" is disrupted by something which lies, ostensibly, "outside" it, and must be brought "in" and when voicing this "otherness" makes a place for the re-enunciating activity of the reader, for the reader's voice.

NOTES

1. Compare an interesting passage from an early letter: "Have you ever noticed that you can often learn more about other people—more about how they feel, how it would feel to be them—by hearing them cough or make one of the innumerable inner noises, than by watching them for hours? Sometimes if another person hiccups, particularly if you haven't been paying much attention to him, why you get a sudden sensation as if you were inside him— you know how he feels in the little aspects he never mentions, aspects which are, really, indescribable to another person and must be realized by that kind of intuition" (to Donald E. Stanford, March 5, 1934; *One Art* 18).

2. In the quoted passage, Alice Quinn notes: "In an early notebook entry, Bishop refers to rhyme as 'mystical,' and throughout her notebooks, her lists and lists of end rhyme words make it clear that she looked to rhyme to drive and refine her intuitive thinking on the basis of the unfettered associations that rhyme yielded up" (273). In a review of Marianne Moore's work published in 1948, Bishop noted that Moore and Edgar Allan Poe "are our two most original writers," and cited Poe's views on originality, noting that, for Poe, it is to be sought in "an extension of the application of the principles of rhyme and alliteration" (*PPL* 684).

3. "*pourquoi tout poète qui ne sait pas au juste combien chaque mot comporte de rimes est incapable d'exprimer une idée quelconque*"; my translation.

4. /pjŏr/, /'pjudər/, /ju/, /jŏ/, according to transcriptions given in the Merriam *Pronouncing Dictionary of American English* (1949), p. 326, 347, 482.

5. Something similar is perhaps at stake in "Sandpiper" (*PPL* 125–126), companion of sorts to "Twelfth Morning" and likewise a text where a "you" appears in the absence of an "I" referred explicitly to the speaker: the pronoun occurs in close proximity to "minute" (/mə 'nju:t/) according to the first pronunciation given in the Merriam *Pronouncing Dictionary of American English* (1949, 281), and "minute," a Blake word, suggests the revelation and coalescence of another way of seeing, more attentive to "particulars."

6. "Rather, it is only when life is attributed to everything that has a history, and not to that which is only a stage setting for history, that [the concept of life] comes into its own" (153).

CHAPTER 6

Causes for Excess: Elizabeth Bishop's Eighty-Eight Exclamations

Christopher Spaide

Abstract Bishop begins her collected poems by calmly distancing her voice from "excitement/as when emotion too far exceeds its cause"; ever since, nearly every review singles out her reticence and her careful measuring of emotion to cause. Yet no list of her most distinctive lines would be complete without her startling exclamations, lines that condense epiphanies and voltas, finally admitted wishes and self-injunctions. And any transcription of her varied orchestration would need to account for screams, cries, and dizzied whoops. Bishop's inimitable voice depends on the occasional excess that, paradoxically, arrives only in precisely controlled circumstances. Bishop's excess in eighty-eight exclamation marks reveals her attraction to personae and secondary voices, and her fascination with the expressive potential of animals and children. Ending on her exceptional "Sonnet," I clarify how that vocal practice changed over her career.

Keywords Excess • Exclamation • Punctuation • Voice • Volume

C. Spaide (✉)
Harvard University, Cambridge, MA, USA

© The Author(s) 2019
A. Cleghorn (ed.), *Elizabeth Bishop and the Music of Literature*,
Palgrave Studies in Music and Literature,
https://doi.org/10.1007/978-3-030-33180-1_6

To my knowledge, no one has ever claimed that Elizabeth Bishop was too loud. No one accuses her of speaking overlong or overemphatically, or charges her with blurting out or chattering on. Bishop herself, certainly, recognized her reputation for reserve. Asked by George Starbuck, at the end of a 1977 *Ploughshares* interview "Cut and occasionally corrected by E. B.," if she would "like to say something mysterious," Bishop answered with a single character:

   ! (Starbuck 11, 29)

When we remember Bishop, we tend to remember not her volume (in any sense) but her reticence, her under- or just-right statement, and her careful measuring of emotion to cause. Those qualities—sometimes understood as the poet's own personality traits, sometimes celebrated as virtues of her work—are singled out in nearly every review and appraisal Bishop has received since her first book *North & South* (1946). Randall Jarrell, in a much-quoted review collected in *Poetry and the Age* (1953), wrote that Bishop's poems "are almost never forced; in her best work restraint, calm, and proportion are implicit in every detail of organization and workmanship." Her subjects merited exclamatory and indignant protest, and yet: "Instead of crying, with justice, 'This is a world in which no one can get along,' Miss Bishop's poems show that it is barely but perfectly possible—has been, that is, for her" (234–235). Bishop and Jarrell could hear and admire those righteous cries bellowed out by their contemporaries—by Robert Lowell, for one, whose tones Bishop once praised as "now-familiar trumpet-notes" (*PPL* 707). If Lowell is a triumphant brass instrument, then perhaps Bishop was a makeshift woodwind, like the "home-made flute" of her alter ego Crusoe, tuned to "the weirdest scale on earth." Yet even Crusoe's instrument could aspire to a particular kind of musical excess, to dizzied whoops: "Home-made, home-made! But aren't we all?" (*PPL* 153).

Bishop is seldom associated with linguistic excess, but she makes it a concern of poems throughout her career, starting with *North & South*'s opening poem "The Map." Whatever else "The Map" may be—an airing of a new poetic voice, a portrait of the poet as a self-cartographer—it is an essay on excess that itself indulges, warily, in excess. In the second and longest of its three stanzas, Bishop underscores the map's excessive displays of language and offers her fanciful explanation:

The names of seashore towns run out to sea,
the names of cities cross the neighboring mountains
—the printer here experiencing the same excitement
as when emotion too far exceeds its cause. (*PPL* 3)

Names meant to order our geography, to designate this town or that city, casually transgress the very boundaries they establish. Doubtless, the names travel farther than our map-reading speaker, as they embark on sea voyages and "cross the neighboring mountains" (as any venturesome Romantic poet should). Whimsically construing linguistic abandon as emotional excess—an imaginative leap taken across the span of an em dash—Bishop turns cartographers and even "the printer" into reckless poets themselves, their control over their language overwhelmed by their "excitement." In apparent contrast with those overexcited mapmakers, Bishop reaffirms her pledge to linguistic exactitude, precisely naming that particular form of "excitement": it arises not from any emotional excess but from an especially excessive excess, an excess that exceeds its cause "too far." And yet Bishop stakes out some linguistic excess of her own. Flattening her voice to a lecturer's careful, repetitive declamation, she strings along assonant, polysyllabic Latinisms ("experiencing," "excitement," "emotion," "exceeds") and lets the loose pentameter of her first lines ease into comfortable prosiness. "The Map" mounts a defense of the aesthetic virtues we most often attribute to Bishop's voice—whimsy, precision, delicacy ("More delicate than the historians' are the map-makers' colors")—but it makes equal room for emotion, excitement, and transgression. A comprehensive cartography of the inner world, Bishop's middle stanza affirms, must map restraint and excess alike.

Considering how early, how explicitly, Bishop brings up the subject of excess—considering, too, that the indulgent printer elicits not admonishment but Bishop's delighting interpretation and giddy imitation—perhaps we ought to listen more closely to Bishop's own excesses of language, volume, and patterning. "The Map" foregrounds excess in its prose rhythms, its extrametrical lines, and its border-crossing place names; for excess on the level of individual words, we could revisit the pratfall-like enjambments of "Arrival at Santos":

Her home, when she is at home, is in Glen Fall
s, New York. (*PPL* 71–72)

Or "Pink Dog":

> Tonight you simply can't afford to be a-
> n eyesore. But no one will ever see a
>
> dog in *máscara* this time of year. (*PPL* 179)

Alternatively, we could listen for her occasional excesses of sonic pattern-ing, an "excess" of "poetic tricks" she reservedly admired in an under-graduate essay on Gerard Manley Hopkins. Whereas Hopkins, combining his tricks with "an intricate sprung rhythm," "keeps them subtle, in vari-ous lights and shades of rhythmical importance" (*PPL* 663), Bishop can redouble internal rhyme, homophones, and assonance for moments of loony humor. Take the uncollected "Exchanging Hats":

> And if the opera hats collapse
> and crowns grow draughty, then, perhaps,
> he thinks what might a miter matter? (*PPL* 199)

Excesses of rhyme, refrain, onomatopoeia, exact and near-repetitions; baroque chains of description, ornamentation, and figuration; explosions out of standard syntax, stanza, and familiar verse-forms: any of these occa-sionally excessive dimensions of Bishop's voice deserves our closer listening.

For the remainder of this chapter, I focus on one especially surprising dimension of that voice: the speech-act of exclamation. In the original poems Bishop collected in book form in her lifetime as well as the four late poems from 1978 to 1979 ("Santarém," "North Haven," "Pink Dog," and "Sonnet"), a total of eighty-eight exclamation marks appear—around one per poem, on average, though they are unevenly distributed, appear-ing in roughly a third of her poems. No one should be surprised to hear that Bishop ranks among her century's least exclamatory poets. Even if you count her poetry's exclamatory animals, every exploding "Boom!" ("Love Lies Sleeping"; *PPL* 13) and thunderous "*Cra-aack!*" ("Electrical Storm"; *PPL* 81), the second section alone of Allen Ginsberg's "Howl" (1956) outshouts Bishop's collected poems by several "holy yells" (139–140). If any punctuation seemed to be Bishop's signature, it might be her question marks, flagging her self-skeptical hypotheses and fleeting caprices; her parentheses, repositories for further observations or hesitant admissions; or the em dashes she often places at beginnings of lines, raised or lowered platforms for shifting her tone up and down.

Still, no list of Bishop's most distinctive lines would be complete without her startling exclamations, lines that condense epiphanies and voltas, finally admitted wishes, and self-injunctions:

>—until everything
> was rainbow, rainbow, rainbow! ("The Fish"; *PPL* 34)
>
> Poor bird, he is obsessed! ("Sandpiper"; *PPL* 126)
>
> Friday was nice.
> Friday was nice, and we were friends.
> If only he had been a woman! ("Crusoe in England"; *PPL* 155)
>
> "Look! It's a she!" ("The Moose"; *PPL* 162)
>
> (*Write* it!) ("One Art"; *PPL* 167)

We tend to underplay Bishop's overstatements, even though the most memorable of these exclamations could serve as synecdoches for entire poems, entire books, even (*Write* it!) for the entirety of Bishop's writing. They deviate, no doubt, from our prevailing perceptive understandings of Bishop—from Seamus Heaney's witty portrait, for instance, of "this most reticent and mannerly of poets," who "usually limited herself to a note that would not have disturbed the discreet undersong of conversation between strangers breakfasting at a seaside hotel" (101). More recently, Gillian White has interpreted Bishop's exclamations as speech acts so blatantly exaggerated, so overdetermined in their exuberant talkiness, that they disrupt the pretense of a coherent lyric "voice" that readers can identify "with an actual person here with them now." And so Bishop's "amplification" of voice in, to take White's example, the climactic realization of "Poem"—"Heavens, I recognize the place, I know it!"—"functions as a metaexpressive moment, even antiexpressive" (81).

What if we imagined that Bishop's exclamations were not anomalies to be puzzled over or written off? What if, instead, we understood them as crucial exercises of an extensive vocal range? Bishop's inimitable voice, I suggest, depends on the occasional exclamation or excessive volume that arrives, paradoxically, only in precisely controlled circumstances. A Bishop poem uses one exclamation mark, sometimes a few (never many more), to establish the outer bound of a voice or emotional predicament, or to transgress those bounds ever so momentarily. Immediately after, Bishop's voice instinctively retreats in the direction of tonal or emotional equilibrium. Only rarely does Bishop open a poem on an exclamation (as in "Filling Station": "Oh, but it is dirty!"); when she does, her poem charts a diminuendo to a softer resolution ("Somebody loves us all") (*PPL* 123–124). And Bishop almost never ends a poem on an exclamation, forgoing any further development or resolution. Though all five famous exclamations quoted above arrive late in their respective poems, and some in the very last stanza or sentence, none sounds its poem's final note. A notable exception comes to mind, and after surveying examples of Bishop's exclamations and their resolutions, from her first book to her last, I will end on that exceptional poem.

Where, in Bishop's early poetry, can we hear excesses of volume, exclamatory language, startling eruptions of sound? Not from her seemingly autobiographical speakers but from the characters and interlocutors, both human and animal, whom those speakers meet. "Alone on the railroad track," the speaker of "Chemin de Fer" (*PPL* 6–7) walks "with pounding heart" but does not translate that pounding heart into pounded-out language. "Chemin de Fer" is Bishop's first poem in ballad stanzas, perfectly rhyming every second and fourth line; the sole formal hint of its speaker's uncertainty is its wavering trimeter, ranging from five to nine syllables in length. (Ingeniously self-referential, Bishop's titular "Chemin de Fer," her run-down railroad, maps out her irregular meter. "The ties were too close together/or maybe too far apart"—just like Bishop's stresses, bunched too close or spaced apart too far.) To articulate her starkest commands, Bishop must first expand the scene—far off, her speaker sees a "little pond ... lie like an old tear/holding onto its injuries/lucidly year after year"—and then introduce a vocal human figure, "the dirty hermit," whose violent actions and exclamations reverberate across that "impoverished" landscape. The poem ends:

> The hermit shot off his shot-gun
>   and the tree by his cabin shook.
> Over the pond went a ripple.
>   The pet hen went chook-chook.
>
> "Love should be put into action!"
>   screamed the old hermit.
> Across the pond an echo
>   tried and tried to confirm it.

This apparent dialogue is really a deluded monologue, the hermit's scream answered by its own echo. Beyond the skepticism condensed in her vainly repetitive phrase, "tried and tried," this speaker keeps her ambivalent silence; she refuses to choose between beckoning, alongside the hermit, that "Love should be put into action!," and seconding that dissenting "echo," *shun, shun, shun*. That chook-chook-ing "pet hen," of all creatures, emerges as the scene's second-most assertive vocal presence—even if Bishop's colloquial verb, "*went* chook-chook," makes the hen's noises seem as mechanical, as purely physical, as the echoing ripple that "went" over the pond.

Animals, in fact, may have the loudest voices in Bishop's early career, none of them quite as raucous as her first book's "Roosters." In a 1940 letter to Marianne Moore, Bishop rebuffed her mentor's drastic revisions to a draft of "Roosters" and defended the poem's extremes: "I can't bring myself to sacrifice what (I think) is a very important 'violence' of tone" (*One Art* 96). To muster that "violence" in the poem's cacophonous first half, she centers every sentence on a word or phrase characterizing the roosters' harsh voices: "the first crow," "echo," "grates," "cries galore," "the uncontrolled, traditional cries," "a senseless order," "gloats" (*PPL* 27). Then, surreally, the roosters' uncontrolled cries coagulate into articulate English speech. Each rooster, "each one," amounts to

> an active
> displacement in perspective;
> each screaming, "This is where I live!"
>
> Each screaming
> "Get up! Stop dreaming!"
> Roosters, what are you projecting? (*PPL* 28)

Bishop—we might reply—what are *you* projecting? None of her other early poems are this insistently exclamatory, this committed to tonal "violence," though Bishop safely displaces violence away from her speaker and onto her English-language roosters. Just as Bishop introduced the "dirty hermit" of "Chemin de Fer" to enunciate, even to "scream," her moral assertions and declarations of unreciprocated "love," in "Roosters" she hands over her boldest directives ("Get up! Stop dreaming!") to "screaming" voices not her own, nor even her own species. Though in certain early poems (such as "The Fish") Bishop's speakers rise to their own exclamation, her animal poems present a different, more oblique approach: self-divided and orchestrated across a chorus of dissimilar vocal ranges.

When, in her third collection *Questions of Travel* (1965), Bishop scores words for other voices, she is readier, riskier, with her exclamations. Increasingly, her poems incorporate languages other than English, comic ventriloquisms, duetting registers and competing volumes. In his remembrance of Bishop, James Merrill shares several anecdotes about traveling to Brazil to visit his favorite living poet; one particularly instructive anecdote shows how casually Bishop orchestrated different moods into different languages. Bishop regularly met with "literary visitors" in Ouro Preto, but Merrill "was her first compatriot to visit in several months," and the first English speaker: "She found it uncanny to be speaking English again." Bishop's other guest at the time was a "young Brazilian painter, in town for the summer arts festival and worn out by long teaching hours." "Late one evening," Merrill remembers,

> over Old-Fashioneds by the stove, a too recent sorrow had come to the surface; Elizabeth, uninsistent and articulate, was in tears. The young painter, returning, called out, entered—and stopped short on the threshold. His hostess almost blithely made him at home. Switching to Portuguese, "Don't be upset, José Alberto," I understood her to say, "I'm only crying in English." (233)

The poems of *Questions of Travel* can cry or cry out, "uninsistent and articulate," in one language, while maintaining their blithe hospitality in another language.

One showpiece for this very sort of vocal conducting is the persona poem. *Questions of Travel* features Bishop's most memorable cast of speakers—some of them eccentric individuals, others identifiable "types," like the tourist or the child—who feel liberated to say what "Bishop," the reticent expatriate poet, would never utter *in propria persona*. As the hectoring patrician talking down to the titular squatter-tenant of "Manuelzinho," Bishop can explore tones of accusation and menace, trying on, rather than describing from a distance, class divisions and indifferent dehumanization: "your children scuttle by me/like little moles aboveground," the speaker snaps, "or even crouch behind bushes/as if I were out to shoot them!" (Lest we ever mistake this speaker for Bishop herself, a prefatory note informs us: "A friend of the writer is speaking" [*PPL 77*].) In "Elsewhere," the second half of *Questions of Travel*, Bishop takes several children, some as rowdy as Manuelzinho's, as her personae. The speaker of "Manners," subtitled "for a Child of 1918," carries her grandfather's etiquette lessons to absurd, ebullient lengths: over the din of automobiles, "we shouted 'Good day! Good day!/Fine day' at the top of our voices" (*PPL* 119). (Other children in "Elsewhere," like the crayon-drawing child of "Sestina," seem unable to shout, let alone speak, at all.) The "loudest" piece in *Questions of Travel*, and the most self-consciously musical, is the symphonic prose of "In the Village," which opens by describing an exclamation not lyric but narrative: "A scream, the echo of a scream, hangs over that Nova Scotian village" (*PPL* 99). If the persona poem allows Bishop to displace her exclamatory impulse, the impressionistic narration of "In the Village" distributes that impulse over the social and natural world. Bishop first harmonizes the "scream" with the "beautiful sounds," "pure and angelic," of the blacksmith's shop, then resolves that scream with the consonance of "the elements speaking: earth, air, fire, water" (*PPL* 100, 118). "Now there is no scream": Bishop's narrator transposes it into her own nostalgic cry, which brings the story to a close: "Oh, beautiful sound, strike again!" (*PPL* 118).

Of the lyrics collected in *Questions of Travel*, none listens to itself more intently, more skeptically, than "The Armadillo" (*PPL* 83–84). In Bonnie Costello's astute condensation, "The Armadillo" begins in a mode of "aesthetic detachment, but a strong moral voice breaks in to oppose the stance of transcendence and aesthetic mastery" (*Questions of Mastery* 75). To recast that progression in terms of volume and tone, "The Armadillo" modulates from warily declarative to explosively odal. Bishop opens with flat, distanced, explanatory indicatives: "This is the time of year/when almost every night/the frail, illegal fire balloons appear." (Today we might recognize these tones from documentary voice-overs; Bishop herself would write in those tones in her Life World Library volume on Brazil.) What spurs Bishop's voice toward its drastic escalation is not the balloons' rise, nor their fiery fall, but the damage inflicted on the defenseless and oblivious fauna below. Speaking as a plural "we"—we the secure humans, we the untroubled observers—Bishop describes three types of animals and their varying attempts to escape. First, "We saw the pair//of owls who nest there," and we registered their motion, color, pattern, and sound: the owls "flying up/and up, their whirling black-and-white/stained bright pink underneath, until" (in a synesthetic conversion of frenzied speed into frantic voice) "they shrieked up out of sight." Next, "Hastily, all alone,/a glistening armadillo left the scene"—not the most mobile animal on this landscape, nor, with its "glistening" armor, the most vulnerable. That would be the third animal, described in a stanza that flaunts Bishop's most devious typographical choices:

> and then a baby rabbit jumped out,
> *short*-eared, to our surprise.
> So soft!—a handful of intangible ash
> with fixed, ignited eyes.

Italicizing "*short*," and punctuating "So soft!" with a hyperventilating exclamation mark and a halting em dash, Bishop's blinkered, impersonally plural speaker announces the shortcomings of a worldview that elevates aesthetic remove over empathic connection. From that perspective, spotting the less common "*short*-eared" breed of rabbit takes precedence over imagining the vulnerability of a "baby" animal, and the rabbit's so-soft!-ness—the rabbit diminished, commodified to fur—earns Bishop's exclamation, not the animal's suffering. Once moral causes are severed from aesthetic effects, local creatures become distantly "intangible," assemblages of already-consumed "ash" and "fixed" eyes that are "ignited" not with inner life but by our haphazardly catastrophic fire.

In a pendulum swing from aesthetic fawning to strained outcry, Bishop follows one vocal extreme with another. The next and final quatrain of "The Armadillo," italicized in full and lifted into a self-consciously poetic register, consists of two end-stopped exclamations:

> *Too pretty, dreamlike mimicry!*
> *O falling fire and piercing cry*
> *and panic, and a weak mailed fist*
> *clenched ignorant against the sky!*

However unprecedented in tone and visual effect, this quatrain reinforces, from an enigmatic and narratively untethered vantage, the whole poem's oppositions between violence and spectacle, pained shrieks, and aesthetic delight. Simply rhyming an agonized "cry" with the danger falling indifferently from the "sky," Bishop corrects the misplaced priorities of her preceding plural speaker. In a cunning false etymology, she tucks that indignant "cry" under an end-word that contains it, "mimi**cry**," as if to suggest that artifice's mimicry can only cover over, not truly answer, a needy, involuntary cry. Corresponding with *The New Yorker* before the poem's magazine publication in 1957, Bishop waffled over this stanza's formatting; she thought it "would look better italicized" and considered leaving off the final exclamation mark—the first exclamation Bishop placed at the end of a mature poem (*The New Yorker* 181). Retaining the exclamation mark, she allows "*piercing cry/and panic*" to instill her final outburst; italicizing the entire stanza, she signals that this voice is not purely her own. That voice resides, rather, in an intersubjective space spanning from "weak mailed" armadillo to detached, judgmental human, and wedged between literary precedents, with Matthew Arnold and the "ignorant armies" of "Dover Beach" on one side and on the other side the cheerful prayer that closes Marianne Moore's own armored-animal poem, "The Pangolin": "'Again the sun!/anew each/day; and new and new and new,/that comes into and steadies my soul'" (144).

By her final collection *Geography III* (1976), Bishop's deployment of exclamations has crystallized into a consistent method. Excepting the Octavio Paz translation "Objects & Apparitions," every poem in this compact book includes an exclamation (sometimes more, three at most) that serves as a center of gravity, if never as an explosive finish: these exclamations are heights to come down from, realizations to be worked out. *Geography III*'s most common exclamation is the imperative to "look," always put to new purposes and precisely pitched in tone. Bishop asks us, variously, to construe the familiar sight of a "Night City" under defamiliarizing figures ("Look! Incandescent,/its wires drip"); to notice the revelatory detail of the "The Moose" ("'Look! It's a she!'"); or to follow the course of an argument, and of a life, in "One Art" ("And look! my last, or/next-to-last, of three loved houses went") (*PPL* 157, 162, 167). Bishop even spoofs these urgings in "12 O'Clock News," when the sight of a typewriter eraser warrants this anthropologist-speaker's breathless yelps: "At last! One of the elusive natives has been spotted!" (*PPL* 164). The sputtered-out climax of "The Moose," an otherwise muted poem, arrives as quoted speech; in other poems, Bishop gives equally dramatic exclamations to her own speakers—the sudden "*oh!* of pain" of "In the Waiting Room," the self-embarrassed discovery of "Poem": "Heavens, I recognize the place, I know it!" (*PPL* 149, 165). When she speaks as "Crusoe in England," Bishop can stretch out her range and voices unrelieved exhilaration and exasperation: "Home-made, home-made! But aren't we all?"; "I got so tired of the very colors!" But just as in her poems voiced *in propria persona*, the highest exclamations of "Crusoe in England" are eventually deflated. Crusoe's hopeless counterfactual "If only he had been a woman!" is definitively closed off by the death, ruefully disclosed at the poem's end, of "Friday, my dear Friday" (*PPL* 153, 154, 155, 156). In "Five Flights Up," the deflation from exclamatory wonder to parenthetical disclosure takes two lines, the book's final couplet: "—Yesterday brought to today so lightly!/(A yesterday I find almost impossible to lift.)" (*PPL* 171). And in "The End of March," Bishop finishes erecting her "crypto-dream-house" and dismantles the entire fantasy in the span of one line: "A light to read by—perfect! But—impossible" (*PPL* 168). Of all the poems in *Geography III*, "One Art" comes closest to ending on an exclamation, with a final stanza that foregrounds speech ("the joking voice"), and a final line whose steely acknowledgment of "disaster" necessitates a typographical double bind—italics and an exclamation mark lend urgency, parentheses hush the self-instruction: "though it may look like (*Write* it!) like disaster" (*PPL* 166). "One Art," whose final punctuation and italics Bishop worked over with Frank Bidart (Fountain and Brazeau 333), implies that exclamation and emphasis are both instrumental to the poetic voice, but neither gets the last word.

The sole exception in Bishop's poetry—the only terminal exclamation mark that is neither quoted nor masked by a persona, neither deflated nor tidily resolved—comes in the last poem she approved for publication, her needle-thin "Sonnet." Punctuation-wise, in fact, "Sonnet" both begins and ends anomalously. Bishop's double-definition poem wields the em dash as a lecture's pointer, indicating the two terms under discussion— "Caught—"; "Freed—" —and the four emblems (two per term) that represent and explain them. Upending traditional sonnet structure, Bishop opens on a sestet, six lines for "Caught," and allows her rapidly developing emblems for "Freed" to run riot through her octave, three lines for her first emblem, five for the second:

> Freed—the broken
> thermometer's mercury
> running away;
> and the rainbow-bird
> from the narrow bevel
> of the empty mirror,
> flying wherever
> it feels like, gay! (*PPL* 180)

What begins as an objective diagram—there are no personal pronouns in "Sonnet," no indications that these emblems are drawn from or confined to a single life—comes into its lyric voice and ends on sincere, full-throated exclamation. With galloping triple rhythms and uninhibited enjambments, this unconventional "Sonnet" heeds Bishop's own advice, "running away" with itself, "flying wherever/it feels like, gay!" Much has been made of the poem's easy-to-read-into final word. "It is impossible to ignore the sexual meaning of 'gay,'" David Mikics notes, "but it would be a mistake to over-emphasize this meaning," to risk "getting in the way of its free flight" (Burt and Mikics 339). To Mikics's point, Bishop saves the poem's most mysterious surprise for last: its terminal exclamation mark. Bishop ends on an exclamation in two other poems: "The Armadillo," and the thoroughly caustic "Pink Dog," with its jeering recommendations: "Dress up! Dress up and dance at Carnival!" (*PPL* 179). In my effort to open up discussion on Bishop's excess in general, I hope to have clarified when and why her voice rises toward exclamation, and how that vocal practice changed over her career. After four full collections whose exclamations ease their pressurized contents but never let them loose, what could announce a "Freed" existence more boldly than a resounding open vowel; an adjective, "gay," that compactly revises an earlier verdict of life as "awful but cheerful"; and then, to end the poem—to end, in fact, Bishop's collected poems—an exclamation?

CHAPTER 7

'A Very Important Violence of Tone': Bishop's 'Roosters' and Other Poems

Thomas Travisano

Abstract This chapter explores ways in which violence of tone served as an important and decisive feature of Bishop's style, beginning at Vassar College and extending through the end of her career. In a college poem such as "A Word with You" (1933), as well as "Roosters" (1941), "The Fish" (1940), "The Armadillo" (1957), "Trouvée" (1968), "In the Waiting Room" (1971), and "Crusoe in England" (1971), Bishop carefully prepares for moments of violence that flash out from a seemingly settled verbal environment. Bishop's technique profoundly influenced the work of her friend and poetic peer Robert Lowell. Despite Bishop's reputation for calm restraint and fastidious perfection, her work is more powerful because of the violence of tone that flashes out of poems at their moments of greatest intensity.

Keywords Bishop • "Roosters," • "The Armadillo," • Violence • Tone

T. Travisano (✉)
Hartwick College, Oneonta, NY, USA

© The Author(s) 2019
A. Cleghorn (ed.), *Elizabeth Bishop and the Music of Literature*,
Palgrave Studies in Music and Literature,
https://doi.org/10.1007/978-3-030-33180-1_7

65

Bishop described to Marianne Moore in their much-discussed October 1940 contretemps over the "sordidities" in Bishop's "Roosters" what she termed a "very important 'violence' of tone." Bishop defended the far-from-polite language in that landmark poem—which she considered her most ambitious so far—because she meant to "emphasize the essential baseness of militarism" (*OA* 96). I would suggest here that this "violence of tone" is by no means limited to "Roosters." Instead, violence of tone served as an important—and even a pervasive—feature of Bishop's style from her days at Vassar College until the end of her career.

Among her mature works, "Roosters" may be a rarity in that this violence of tone emerges very early. It is hinted at even in the "gun-metal blue dark" and "gun-metal blue windows" of the poem's first two stanzas (*PPL* 27). And then that violence steadily escalates until it becomes for many stanzas the poem's dominant feature. This unsettling intensity is partly what drew Moore's apprehension and has attracted the notice of readers ever since. Indeed, the intensity, sometimes approaching brutality, that pervades the first 26 stanzas of "Roosters" may tempt some readers to overlook the gentleness, understatement, and delicate beauty of the poem's five closing stanzas. More commonly, however, in Bishop's mature writing, that important violence of tone does not dominate most of a given poem's length. Instead, it emerges swiftly and suddenly out of a predominant stream of controlled and understated diction. It makes its dramatic—and indelible—impact. Then it folds itself back into the understated stream.

I began to be aware of just how pervasive and important this suddenly emerging violence, tonal violence, is to Bishop's writing while at work on a forthcoming biography of the poet. As I closely studied the poems Bishop was producing at Vassar, I found that in these experimental and perhaps not-quite-fully-successful poems, a tone that sometimes seems to border on verbal pommeling is often a conspicuous—and sometimes even a predominant—feature of her style. If I've learned one thing from my years of reading and rereading Bishop's poetry, it is that once Bishop had gained command of a particular technique or tonal feature, she never forgot it. She would continue to deploy such a technique in later writing, often in ways that are by no means easy to see or to define. For example, after the early explorations of surrealism that were crucial to her college and post-college years, flashes of what Bishop later termed "the always more successful surrealism of everyday life" (*PPL* 861) continue to emerge even in poems that might be deemed among her most "objective" or "realistic."

Once I began to look over the whole of Bishop's work for further evidence of her deployment this important, if sometimes fleeting, violent tone, I began to find it almost everywhere—flashing out briefly but effectively in poem after poem. This chapter will show by reference to a few examples chosen among many technical mechanisms by which Bishop makes "violence of tone" a significant—and sometimes even a decisive—feature of her style. It will thereby show how important these flashes of violence are to the emotional and thematic development of several of her most intriguing and compelling works.

My Exhibit A is the ending of Bishop's 1957 masterwork "The Armadillo." Bishop begins by describing with singular delicacy a Brazilian scene witnessed from the mountaintop home at Samambaia that Bishop shared with her lover Lota de Macedo Soares. Here she watches "frail, illegal fire balloons.../climbing the mountain's height." They are illegal because of the danger they represent to the forest and houses below as a result of the flaming jellied gasoline that fuels them, but they steal one's heart because of their beauty as they steer gracefully "between/the kite sticks of the Southern Cross//receding, dwindling, solemnly//and steadily forsaking us" (*PPL* 83). It's all fun and games until "the downdraft from a peak" sucks one of the fire balloons down forcefully against the granite cliff that towers over the Samambaia house. This errant fire balloon, whose flaming fuel acts very much like napalm, splatters "like an egg of fire/against the cliff behind the house." When "The flames ran down," the jellied petroleum clings to the trees and sets off a massive conflagration in the forest below. A pair of familiar nesting owls "shriek up out of sight," confronting the viewer and the reader with a definite tone of violence. In terms of the poem's handling of tone, what should particularly attract one's attention is the penultimate stanza, in which Bishop moves with extraordinary deftness, even within a single line, from a tone of extraordinary gentleness to a tone almost of rage, as suddenly a "baby rabbit jump[s] out" of the burning forest:

> *short*-eared, to our surprise.
> So soft!—a handful of intangible ash
> with fixed, ignited eyes. (*PPL* 102)

Let's walk through these three lines step by step. What could seem gentler or more tender than a fluffy baby bunny? But why is this bunny so surprisingly "*short*-eared"? Can it be that its long ears have been *burned off* by the illegal blaze? Why does this rabbit, which one wants to reach out and cradle in one's hand, seem like "a handful of intangible ash"? Is it only because of the rabbit's plush fur, or is its body literally turning to ash while being consumed by the flames? The rabbit's "fixed, ignited eyes"—these, at least, are so far intact—seem themselves to be on fire as they reflect (like a deer in the headlights) the man-made fire that surrounds them and obliterates their world. Of special note is the way the poem slips in mid-sentence, or even in midline, from a tone of ambiguous and bemused, if subverted gentleness toward a tone of shocked horror in the face of such destruction. The word "*short*" in the hyphenated "*short*-eared" is italicized and the word soft receives a mid-sentence exclamation mark. This anticipates the final stanza, with its forceful, violent tone, is punctuated by exclamatory sentences that are italicized in their entirety.

> *Too pretty, dreamlike mimicry!*
> *O falling fire and piercing cry*
> *and panic, and a weak mailed fist*
> *clenched ignorant against the sky!*

The intensity of this closing stanza might almost seem uncharacteristic of its author, yet it has raised few objections even among readers who prize Bishop for her delicacy. Perhaps this is because the violent closing has been so subtly and effectively prepared. The poem indeed builds gradually from delicacy toward violence throughout its course, and particularly in the poem's remarkably managed final stanzas.

Robert Lowell was deeply impressed when he read "The Armadillo" in typescript, describing it to Bishop in a June 10, 1957, letter as "surely one of your three or four very best" (*WIA* 204). Three years later he confessed "I carry 'The Armadillo' in my billfold and occasionally amaze people with it" (*WIA* 324). He was so taken with the poem that Bishop dedicated it to him when it was later collected in her 1965 volume *Questions of Travel.* Lowell's earlier style is noted for its sustained—and sometimes almost overwhelming—violence of tone, which Bishop termed in her *Life Studies* blurb as his "now-familiar trumpet-notes" (*WIA* 289). Lowell's signature early poem, his 1947 "Quaker Graveyard in Nantucket," begins with violent force and carries that momentum all the way through to the end, with only the sixth section, the quietly reverent "Our Lady of Walsingham," affording contrast (*Collected Poems* 17). As Lowell's work approached crisis a decade later, he found a more subtle and modulated way to incorporate elements of violence into his work in Bishop's "Armadillo," which he acknowledged to be the model for his own most popular poem, "Skunk Hour." Bishop's

"Armadillo" revealed to Lowell a technique of modulation, a means of shifting gears with an almost-seamless alternation between an understated lyric or prosy evenness and something more violent, sudden, and aggressive. It is no wonder that Lowell was particularly drawn to this poem. Lowell offers a deliberate echo of Bishop's "Armadillo" when he locates the "moonstruck eyes' red fire" of his titular skunks in the exact location—the penultimate stanza—as Bishop's short-eared rabbit's "fixed, ignited eyes." Significantly, while Bishop's poem ends all in italics with its exclamatory stanza of violent protest, Lowell's ends much more bemusedly. The threat it offers is looming and ambiguous, as mother skunk and her kits seek supper from the backyard garbage pail. Certainly, italics would have had no place in Lowell's effectively understated closing. In Kay Jamison's important new study of Lowell, she characterizes Lowell in her title as *Setting the River on Fire*. But it was Bishop's "Armadillo" that added to Lowell's bag of tricks as he observed her quite literally *setting the forest on fire*.

I've begun with "The Armadillo" and explored it in detail because it shows how skillfully, in mid-career, Bishop had mastered the art of making moments of savagery flash out from a quieter background. A rather earlier example, from 1940, is a poem that was for a long time her most famous: "The Fish." After its prosy, economically descriptive opening, the poem begins to gather intensity as it moves toward an interior view of her "tremendous" catch—a gigantic jewfish (*WIA* 71), a species that can grow to 400 pounds or more and that has now been appropriately renamed the Goliath Grouper. Bishop's tour of this big-jawed grouper's innards is prefaced and framed by a reference to a potential source of unnerving violence: "the frightening gills,/fresh and crisp with blood,/that can cut so badly." The poem quickly averts its gaze from this gashing source of danger, yet the succeeding lines remain more than a little unsettling, in their never quite matter-of-fact detail:

> I thought of the coarse white flesh
> packed in like feathers,
> the big bones and the little bones,
> the dramatic reds and blacks
> of his shiny entrails,
> and the pink swim-bladder
> like a big peony. (*PPL* 33)

A sharp violence of tone flashes out again at the end of the poem with the "grim, wet, and weaponlike" hooks whose lines and leaders are trailing from the ancient fish's large and aching jaw. Only after the aggressive act of hooking a fish has been confronted can the poem move to its culminating and ecstatic "rainbow, rainbow, rainbow!" And the rainbow itself is the product of the oil in the boat's bilge, itself a potentially toxic presence in a natural environment.

As we have already seen in "The Armadillo" and "The Fish," in many of her poems violence is displaced onto how humans consciously or unconsciously observe animals—and, as we have already seen in several examples, brutal moments often emerge in surprising and disconcerting ways. For example, in the 1968 "Trouvée," the poet is startled by the conundrum of confronting a chicken left flattened on the roadway in Greenwich Village by a passing automobile:

> Oh, why should a *hen*
> have been run over
> on West 4th Street
> in the middle of summer?

This deceased but not departed creature confronts the poet-speaker as a disconcerting form of found art (or *trouvée*), transformed by a passing motorist from living entity into a disturbing abstraction:

> She was a white hen
> –red-and-white now, of course.
> How did she get there?
> Where was she going?
>
> Her wing feathers spread
> flat, flat in the tar,
> all dirtied, and thin
> as tissue paper.

Part of the shock confronting the observer is that a flattened chicken can't be readily explained in this urban environment, where chickens rarely range freely:

> A pigeon, yes,
> or an English sparrow,
> might meet such a fate,
> but not that poor fowl. (*PPL* 141)

Another guilt-provoking element of disquiet is that a crushed sparrow or pigeon would not have made a trouvée, and thus the subject for a poem, because of the death of these grayish birds in a city is just too common and because of the absence of the intriguing color contrast, with the dramatic "red-and-white" turning only gradually toward a dirtied, thinning gray. This poem's aspect of violence is muted and almost, but not quite, subsumed into a wry, self-deprecatory irony. The poem contains within it a knowledge of the ongoing threats to life and limb (or wing) that are part of the workaday urban world, here an automotive pommeling of one of nature's creatures that the driver who flattened the "poor fowl" into a disquieting *trouvée* may even have been oblivious of. The poem takes the flattened bird as its piece of found art even as it serves as this particular pullet's singular elegy and memorial.

A few flashes of violence emerge from the boarding school poems that graced *The Blue Pencil* during Bishop's Walnut Hill School years from 1927 to 1930. However, it was in the anonymous poems Bishop contributed to Vassar's renegade alternative magazine *Con Spirito*—which Bishop cofounded and edited with such friends as Mary McCarthy, Frani Blough Muser, and Eleanor Clark—that she began experimenting in earnest with that "very important 'violence' of tone" which she offered to Marianne Moore in defense of "Roosters." An edge of violence—and sometimes a good deal more than an edge—may be found in nearly all the published work Bishop produced in her college years, where this fierceness of tone is often interwoven with a surreal humor. Significantly, even in these poems, which Bishop composed in her early 20s, this sometimes-savage tone is often explored through connections to the animal world. In 1953, Bishop praised the "undiminished un-pulled punch" of Lowell's "Words for Hart Crane" (*WIA* 140). And there are certainly no pulled punches in the opening of Bishop's own experimental 1933 effort, "A Word with You":

> Look out! there's that damned ape again
> sit silently until he goes,
> or else forgets the things he knows
> (whatever they are) about us, then
> we can begin to talk again.

But talk in this zoo-like atmosphere with an auditor who appears to be the speaker's intimate friend is difficult because, as the poem continues:

> —Oh Lord, what's the use,
> for now the parrot's after me
> and the monkeys are awake. You see
>
> how hard it is, you understand
> this nervous strain in which we live—
> Why just one luscious adjective
> infuriates the whole damned band
> and they're squabbling for it. (*PPL* 190)

The vehement tone established in the opening and that continues in the lines above—as the danger of being overheard in intimate conversation and perhaps being mocked, bullied, or jeered for using even "one luscious adjective"—continues through the entire poem. One thing that puzzled me until recently about "A Word with You" was how to locate and understand the situation of the speaker. Here, clearly, were zoo animals. But was the discomfited speaker inside or outside the cage with the zoo creatures, and how could the ape, parrots, and monkeys actually be listening, since one might presume that they don't understand human speech? However, in a recent seminar at Hartwick College, my students had no difficulty parsing the situation. These students understood that Bishop wrote the poem while living in a Vassar dormitory, and they confidently explained to their eagerly listening teacher that Bishop had captured in words an essential feature of student life at a small liberal arts college, the experience of living in a fishbowl—or as this poem more aptly puts it, a zoo—where all one says or does may be witnessed or overheard, and perhaps even mocked, jeered at, or gossiped about by one's fellow inmates, in the dining halls, dorms, classrooms, and public areas of the college. In such a setting, one's every move may be watched and commented on by the human equivalents of apes and parrots. And one's attempts at intimacy, or even of a few sentences of intelligent conversation with a friend, become the targets of chatter, gossip, or scorn. In such a setting, even getting in, as the poem's title has it, "a word with you" might offer a considerable challenge. The abrupt and violent diction of the poem captures that feeling of being watched, harassed, and parroted.

> Quick! there's the cockatoo! he heard!
> (He can't bear any form of wit.)
> —Please watch out that you don't get bit;
> there's not a thing escapes that bird.
> Be silent,—now the ape has overheard. (*PPL* 190)

No wonder, then, that Bishop and her fellow authors chose to meet to perform their editorial work on *Con Spirito* in a nearby speakeasy and that they chose, as well, not to sign their names to their literary productions in that short-lived but influential little magazine.

Even in this very early poem, written almost a quarter century before "The Armadillo," Bishop is already performing many of the linguistic tricks that made that later poem's last two stanzas work so tellingly. These techniques include more than one midline (or mid-sentence) exclamation point as well as mid-sentence or even pre-sentence dashes. Indeed, Bishop's persistent use of unconventional punctuation throughout the poem's opening stanza and its subsequent lines serve to create a violently syncopated staccato rhythm that supports the poem's theme and mood and that remains worthy of careful study. Bishop's later skirmishes with the punctilious grammarians on *The New Yorker*'s copy-editing staff over her frequent violations of punctuational niceties—such as we have already noted in "The Armadillo"—could be anticipated by her practice in such early work as "A Word with You." In fairness to *The New Yorker*, however, it must be noted that in the case of "The Armadillo" her unusual punctuation of the penultimate stanza was accepted without cavil and that the magazine also readily agreed to her *post*-submission suggestion that the entire final stanza be italicized (*New Yorker* 180–182).

Immediate and abrupt violence of tone, which persists through unsettling images in "The Burglar of Babylon," "Crusoe in England," "Pink Dog," and "A Drunkard," may also be recognized in such earlier Vassar productions as the brashly, even bizarrely, comic mock-tribute "Hymn to the Virgin," as well as in "Some Dreams They Forgot," and in the first and third of her "Three Valentines," which—after first appearing in Vassar publications—reappeared, along with "The Reprimand" in the 1935 anthology *Trial Balances*, a volume in which several of Bishop's earliest efforts were graced by an introduction by Marianne Moore's. Moore there took note of Bishop's "methodically oblique, intent way of working" and her capacity for "the kind of refraction that is peculiar to works of art."[1] One signature that appeared in *Trial Balances*, then did not appear again in print until 11 years later, when it became the lead poem of *North & South*. This poem was Bishop's "The Map." This is rightly seen as one of Bishop's signature poems, not only for its self-defining geographical theme but also for its cool, seemingly detached and "methodically oblique" ironies and layered complexities of tone. The sudden emergence of a mature style in Bishop's "The Map" has always seemed a kind of miracle to me. And it now seems even more miraculous to me—arising from the sea as it does almost like Botticelli's radiant yet tranquil Venus out of the context of the roiling sequence of verbal assaults so characteristic of much of her college work.

Yet, as I've already suggested, that violence of tone with which Bishop was experimenting in the writing just before she developed her mature style never really disappeared from her artistic palette. Indeed, it always remained among a range of bright primary colors which frequently found their place in Bishop's verbal portraits and landscapes. One of Bishop's most compelling late landscape poems, which is also a masterpiece of verbal portraiture, is "Crusoe in England." This poem is marked by more than a few sharp flashes of verbal assault, and it carries forward the links between violence and the animal motif. As the poem begins, a new volcano is witnessed as it rises hissing from the sea. Later we encounter hissing turtles, hissing lava, hissing rain, and the "*shriek, shriek, shriek/baa ... shriek ... baa*" (*PPL* 154) of the gulls and goats that overrun this Crusoe's tenuous island home, and that are reminiscent in their way of the shrieking owls of "The Armadillo." But the poem's most violent moment flows out of the context of more pleasant dreams in the form of a recurrent nightmare:

> But then I'd dream of things
> like slitting a baby's throat, mistaking it
> for a baby goat. I'd have
> nightmares of other islands
> stretching away from mine, infinities
> of islands, islands spawning islands,
> like frogs' eggs turning into polliwogs
> of islands.... (*PPL* 155)

Crusoe's dreams, stoked in part by his "awful, fizzy, stinging" alcoholic "home-brew," are nightmares of a life and world spinning suddenly and violently out of control.

Volcanoes are a dominant feature of Crusoe's landscape (he has 52 of them), and volcanoes make an appearance, too, in Bishop "In the Waiting Room," a poem that begins quietly and claustrophobically, but that erupts suddenly with violent force from the pages of *The National Geographic*. Emerging from those closely studied pages the child-speaker sees:

> the inside of a volcano,
> black, and full of ashes;
> then it was spilling over
> in rivulets of fire.

She also witnesses a figure who is soon to be cannibalized:

A dead man slung on a pole
—"Long Pig," the caption said.

And she discovers as well in the *Geographic*'s pages exotic-seeming babies
and their women—members of a culture whose foreignness cannot be
readily accounted for in the child's staid and overcoated winter confine-
ment in Puritanical Worcester, Massachusetts:

Babies with pointed heads
wound round and round with string;
black, naked women with necks
wound round and round with wire
like the necks of light bulbs.
Their breasts were horrifying. (*PPL* 149)

Much of the poem's force arises from its powerful modulations between a
sense of enclosure and the literally dizzying release from that enclosure—
almost with the effect of a volcanic eruption—into something ineluctably
different from anything she has known. The child in the poem links her
dawning recognition of her own identity to her own seemingly inexplica-
ble connection to the human community—"you are an *I,*/you are an
Elizabeth,/you are one of *them*" (*PPL* 150). The poem's confrontation
between sameness and otherness, between the self and the unaccountably
external, is supported and intensified by the emergence at key moments of
a "very important violence of tone."

We are now prepared to return to October 1940, when Bishop was
finalizing her poem "Roosters" even as she was confronting reports from
the European and Asian battlefronts that marked the opening years of the
Second World War. As she digested these reports, Bishop was confronting
what she described to Moore as "the essential baseness of militarism," and
she was linking her refusal to accept all that this militarism implied with
the reminders she heard through their crowing every morning of the hun-
dreds of carefully cultivated fighting cocks that then formed an unavoid-
able element of the social fabric of Key West, where Bishop had chiefly
resided over the past several years. As she searched for resources to turn
her intuitions into words, Bishop found one in the violence of tone that
had predominated in her experimental Vassar College style, which was
then only a few years in her past. And she made this violent tone the

unmistakably dominant characteristic of the opening of "Roosters." Here, too, Bishop has created a poem where animals are closely associated with human machismo, which may be noted in particular in the bright, assertive, and often *primary* colors, of its violent male titular birds:

> The crown of red
> set on your little head
> is charged with all your fighting blood.
>
> Yes, that excrescence
> makes a most virile presence,
> plus all that vulgar beauty of iridescence. (*PPL* 28–29)

These militaristic roosters have been trained to fight and even kill one another by their cock-fighting masters, and they carry out their battles in an effort for what the poem suggests is a fleeting and futile search for self-assertion and glory:

> Now in mid-air
> by twos they fight each other.
> Down comes a first flame-feather,
>
> and one is flying,
> with raging heroism defying
> even the sensation of dying.

Perhaps there is courage and even a kind of terrible beauty to be found in the conflict of roosters, but their crowing and their fighting also creates social disruption and leads ultimately to an ignominious death for not a few combative roosters.

> And one has fallen,
> but still above the town
> his torn-out, bloodied feathers drift down;
>
> and what he sung
> no matter. He is flung
> on the gray ash-heap, lies in dung
>
> with his dead wives
> with open, bloody eyes,
> while those metallic feathers oxidize. (*PPL* 29)

Stripped of his "green-gold medals" and deprived of a hero's funeral, this rash and bloodied rooster is simply discarded. The rooster's "open, bloodied eyes" might just imply the creature's final, shocked recognition that militaristic postures are not only base but empty—and that they may in the end prove lethal to the militarist himself.

The drifting, bloodied flame-feathers offer a moment of surreal, disturbing calm in the context of these roosters' violent world. As such, "Roosters" almost might be seen as pushing the comic and figurative conflict of Stevens' "Bantams in Pine-woods" to another level—toward a level that is all-too-disturbingly literal. From her college years onward—Bishop deployed violence of tone as one of the primary colors in her artistic palette. Most often, in her mature work, she allowed herself only flashes of violence at just the right moment. But in the 1940 "Roosters," faced with a flaring of militarism that had already consumed much Europe and Asia, and that would soon threaten to consume North America as well, Bishop made her exploration of tonal aggression a dominant element in a poem that remains one of her finest.

NOTE

1. Marianne Moore, *Complete Prose*, ed. Patricia Willis. (New York: Penguin, 1986, 329).

CHAPTER 8

"Spontaneity occurs in a good *attack*": Voice Control in Late Bishop

Angus Cleghorn

Abstract Bishop's shifts in tone are sometimes subtle and at other times erratic. I am interested in two coincidental effects: shifts in poetic form (meter, rhythm, speech), together with signals of cultural identification. Voiced syntax and cultural signals reach readers with musical shifts (such as alterations from blank verse to prosaic voices) that lead up to such voiced interjections. These gongs in Bishop's work, odd and humorous utterances, while jarring, also bring the reader into the poem through recognition of cultural echoes. Exclamations disrupt traditional reading experiences of the sublime and authentic; moments of cultural debasement initially appear to mar or de-authenticate poetry. In this process Bishop portrays late twentieth-century culture's turn away from traditional artforms. This innovative otherness registers different cultural markers of global identities.

Keywords Bishop • Voice • Tone • Poetic form • Music • Identity

A. Cleghorn (✉)
Seneca College, Toronto, ON, Canada

© The Author(s) 2019
A. Cleghorn (ed.), *Elizabeth Bishop and the Music of Literature*,
Palgrave Studies in Music and Literature,
https://doi.org/10.1007/978-3-030-33180-1_8

Elizabeth Bishop's shifts in tone are sometimes subtle and at other times erratic. I am interested in two coincidental effects: shifts in poetic form (meter, rhythm, speech), together with signals of cultural identification (and sometimes the two work in dialogic reverberation within poems). These shifts within poems occur within many forms and always entail changes in voice, sometimes abruptly raising the reader's eyebrows, and other times subtly modifying poetic form in the poem's rhythmic action and imagery.

Many of her late poems follow a pattern of development that renovates twentieth-century poetics: an iambic pentameter base undergoes rhythmical variation, loosening up the poem for surprisingly diverse rhetorical intonation, which leads into prosaic verse. While Vidyan Ravinthiran has demonstrated how the poems modulate from traditional iambic forms to contemporary prose in *Elizabeth Bishop's Prosaic*, and Christopher Spaide's chapter investigates Bishop's exclamations, I am particularly interested here in Bishop's breaks—that is, her utterances that shift rhetorical intonation and in so doing point to cultural variations. These other perspectives are enabled by polyphonic poetry, which simultaneously signals changes in voice and form (and sometimes even appears to act as poetics commenting on poetry's evolution at hand).

Here are some examples that tend to occur suddenly and surprisingly: in "The Fish" after the epiphanic rainbow of victory ironized by oil, "then I let the fish go." In "Santarém," the "church/(Cathedral, rather!)" had "been struck by lightning," as was "The priest's house right next door//*Graças a deus*—he'd been in Belém," and then the poetic speaker enters the "blue pharmacy" and receives the gift of a "small, exquisite, clean matte white" wasps' nest only to have "Mr. Swan,/Dutch, the retiring head of Philips Electric,/really a very nice old man,/who wanted to see the Amazon before he died,/[ask] 'What's that ugly thing?" There's also the subtle downturn at the end of "Edgar Allan Poe & the Juke-Box" when after countering Poe's "*exact*" poetics with her mechanical pleasures, the speaker asks, "how long does the music burn?/like poetry, or all your horror/half as exact as horror here?" Much more horrific is "A Drunkard," in which the speaker remembers as a three-year-old witnessing the Great Salem Fire; she "picked up a woman's long black cotton/stocking. Curiosity. My mother said sharply/*Put that down!*" and since that reprimand she "suffered from abnormal thirst—/I swear it's true" confesses the alcoholic only to conclude "I'm half-drunk now ..../And all I'm telling you may be a lie" (*PPL* 253).

Lorrie Goldensohn finds this "an awkward narrator" causing the poem to yield "to a kind of smirking comedy" (*Cambridge Companion* 193) that does not measure up to more accomplished "changes of register" that are "pure gifts," such as the Baptist seal in "At the Fishhouses," and "*Write it!*" in "One Art." These latter moments though self-conscious assert sublimity and therefore re-establish traditional poetic heights, albeit with postmodern reflexivity. Goldensohn successfully argues that "A Drunkard" as a poetic draft lacks the polish of Bishop's masterpieces, yet I suggest that what might also bother her is what bothers many readers of a poem such as "Santarém." Bishop in "A Drunkard" like Mr. Swan in "Santarém" is being a party pooper. They are de-authenticating the sincerity of the poetic experience. Perhaps by letting in this type of disruptive bullshit, Bishop is registering crass late twentieth-century culture. Mr. Swan's bucket list mentality demonstrates the capitalist attempting to consume the world, in this case the Amazon, while he still can; in "A Drunkard" Bishop's alcoholic narrator is unreliable. But perhaps this unreliability ultimately reveals more of the alcoholic's twisted sincerity than insincerity. She is admitting that she may well be inflating her memory emotionally, and this makes alcoholic sense, for many readers find the weight of the maternal reprimand in the poem to melodramatically exceed its cause and its traumatic affect. It's a case of emotional excess in art like that of Hamlet as charged by T. S. Eliot.[1] So we have a sticky situation here in late Bishop: modernist standards of bad art and bad taste become part of the art. Does this lessen it? I suggest that it does not because in these cases the poems modulate so much that we can compare and contrast various artistic registers. And with that, we also get a lot of late twentieth-century debasement in works that still carry forward some lingering effects of sublimity. Sweet and sour flavors enable us to taste both.

In a 1995 essay from *The Wallace Stevens Journal* special issue on Stevens and Bishop, George Lensing writes about "The Way a Poet Should See, The Way a Poet Should Think": "she typically and rather quickly grows self-conscious of such elevated formality and likes nothing better than to interrupt it with the intrusion of a self-doubting question, a corrective rephrasing, or a bathetic reversal" (128). Bathos is defined in the *OED* as a "fall from sublime to commonplace; anti-climax; performance absurdly unequal to occasion." Such bad behavior is on display in the anticlimax of "A Drunkard's" lie.

So Lensing partially precurses the call of Eleanor Cook on the first page of *Elizabeth Bishop at Work* "about exactly how does she did it, this master poet of the twentieth century" (1). In showing "people trying to orient themselves in strange conditions" (214), Bishop has often been noted for successfully rendering the other. Think of "Manuelzinho," for example, and the way this other and his hilarious phrases are part of the poetic voice together with Lota de Macedo Soares. She, "*A friend of the writer is speaking*" about "the world's worst gardener since Cain" (*PPL 77*), who brings her "a pumpkin 'bigger than the baby.'" Readers hear Manuelzinho's voice quoted amid the indignantly amused narration of Lota as written by Bishop. It is a study of class differences through these three characters' judgmental comments and actions. As the narrator observes, "I watch you through the rain,/trotting, light, on bare feet,/up the steep paths you have made—/or your father and grandfather made—/all over my property," the long-established class relationship between Lota and Manuelzinho's families endures until the speaker says, "I can't endure it/ another minute; then,/indoors, beside the stove,/keep on reading a book" (77). Would Lota be so bothered by this, and would she be the cook with a book? This persona is more likely Bishop.[2] At several junctures, the poet's perspective is woven into Lota's narrative view of Manuelzinho; this three-in-one merger of identities keeps readers attuned to modulations in class and character. Another example occurs toward the end of the poem at dusk: "Between us float a few/big, soft, pale-blue,/ sluggish fireflies,/the jellyfish of the air" (80). There are no quotation marks to coin the jellyfish as Manuelzinho's creative commentary. The metaphor sounds like it could be his or Lota's sense of humor, and yet the beauty of this image sounds like Bishop looking at fireflies in "A Cold Spring," or using the pale-blue morpho butterfly in "Anjinhos," her collage box inspired by Joseph Cornell. Then the tender, empathic humor of the poet imagines Manuelzinho's mother teaching him to paint his straw hat before the friend of the writer reportedly said, "Unkindly,/I called you the Klorophyll Kid./My visitors thought it was funny./I apologize here and now." This is surely Lota, but then the last stanza expresses her love supposedly while saying "I take off my hat, unpainted/and figurative, to you./Again I promise to try." This exchanged hat figuratively tipped to Manuelzinho is the poem's departing and signature gesture. As such, the exchanged hat comes from Bishop as poet more so than Lota, the friend of the writer whose landownership has been translated into Bishop's poem. Within these subtle transgressions of voice, identity, and class, we observe the manners in human interactions that delineate character (there are also the extremely funny examples, such as Manuelzinho's "Dream

Books" for accounting, or his use of Lota's money to hire a bus "for the delighted mourners") (78).

Eleanor Cook's chapter eight, in particular the section on tone is most probing in subtle analysis of Bishop's innovative tonal techniques. Cook builds upon observations from Lowell, Swenson, Frost, Heaney, and Eliot (all aural poets) and quotes James Merrill on a key factor: "Manners are for me the touch of nature, an artifice in the very bloodstream. Someone who does not take them seriously is making a serious mistake. ... And manners—whether good or bad—are entirely allied with tone or voice in poetry" ("An Interview with Donald Sheehan," 33; Cook 223). Consider Bishop's poem "Manners" and how her grandfather teaches politeness to the extent that young Bishop treats Willy and the crow with the utmost respect, only to have automobiles drive by and leave them and their horse-drawn carriage in the dust while shouting, "Good Day! Good Day!/Fine Day! at the top of [their] voices." This is a form of embarrassment that we Canadians revel in, a kind of humility and dignity that for most of us takes priority over the denigrating shame a proud American might feel here. Note that Bishop depicts her seven-year-old self in a state of innocence learning this lesson of humility and grace from her grandfather who embodies a more mannered past. Their voices register manners after the poetic scene is established carefully with both sides—rural, slow, polite Nova Scotia and automated, fast, rude commuters.

But it's what Merrill says about "an artifice in the very bloodstream" that indicates what Bishop does so well. Recall the artifice of "A Drunkard's" lie, and Mr. Swan's insulting "ugly thing." These voices register disso-nances from the dominant tones in each poem so much so that their discords almost sound artificial. However, each poem's interjection of apparent inauthenticity ultimately registers a more complex, sincerely rich experi-ence. Bishop makes the fake real. She describes a similar effect in "Writing poetry is an unnatural act...": The poet's goal is to "convince himself (per-haps, with some luck, eventually some readers) that what he's up to and what he's saying is really an inevitable, *only* natural way of behaving under the circumstances" (*PPL* 702). Bishop concludes her talk from the late 1950s, early 1960s by referring to her "Grandmother's Glass Eye," which has reflected much critical understanding of Bishop's poetics: "the problem of writing poetry ... the difficulty of combining the real with the decidedly un-real; the natural with the unnatural; the curious effect a poem produces of being as normal as *sight* and yet as synthetic, as artificial, as a *glass eye* ... spontaneity occurs in a good *attack*, a rapid line, *tight* rhythm" (706).

To move from the apparently real to "the decidedly un-real," Bishop often jars readers as we have seen. Sometimes she slows down this process to make it seem inevitable and natural. In Nova Scotia, Bishop experienced *"Everyday and Its Underside,"* as Cook labels her book's next section after tone, and which offers "The Moose" as a wonderful example of speech, tone, social landscape, the underside of everyday, as well as the sublime. We might consider "At the Fishhouses" as another example already covered adeptly in this book. If we go back a bit, we can trace how Bishop gets the underside of everyday into her poetry after being an undergraduate at Vassar dazzled by Stevens, having memorized *"Harmonium* almost by heart" (Lensing 117). As her poetry developed from *North & South* to *A Cold Spring,* she "fought the battle of the iambic pentameter" (Cook 1), thus updating twentieth-century poetics. Vidyan Ravinthiran has success-fully shown how *Elizabeth Bishop's Prosaic* achieves this by altering iambic lines with prose rhythms. George Lensing had previously quoted Bishop's dislike for the way Stevens makes "blank verse moo," and critics such as Penelope Laurans and John Hollander helped develop her technical evolu-tion in poems with subtle variations on blank verse such as "Cape Breton."

Another sublime coastline poem written later that expresses the every-day, its underside, the real and decidedly unreal, as well as a dialogue with Stevens, is "The End of March" (*PPL* 167–169). This poem performs some rhythmical unearthing in its transformative prosody. The regular iam-bic gait of "to take a walk on that long beach" is surrounded by other tetrameter lines until pentameter spills over: "indrawn: the tide far out, the ocean shrunken," its excessive syllable then recoils in the short, literal next line, "seabirds in ones or twos." It's as though Bishop is counting more than the birds here, and also their rhythm in the lyric. The second stanza reestablishes regular iambic tetrameter with "The sky was darker than the water," only to have it elongated with sea breakers: "lengths and lengths, endless, of wet white string,/looping up to the tide-line, down to the water,/over and over. Finally, they did end"—even that last line has 11 syl-lables as it marks the end of the seemingly endless rolling waves. Then when Bishop writes of "giving up the ghost" in the next lines, I wonder if that's "the spirit" "fluttering its empty sleeves" who "sang beyond the genius of the sea" in Stevens' predominantly iambic exorcism of the poetic muse, "The Idea of Order at Key West." Bishop learned from Stevens to give up the ghost in the "common myth-kitty" of modern poetry, as Larkin described it. And as Bonnie Costello and Harold Bloom have remarked, "The End of March" is a dialogue with Stevens and his majestic lion sun.

Bishop makes her own poetic abode first stylistically by altering the iambic lines (and setting the meter into reflexive dialogue with rhythmical variations in the poem, which are emphasized by imagery), and then to accompany her own constructions, she builds her "proto-dream-house," uniquely "a sort of artichoke of a house, but greener (boiled with bicarbonate of soda?)," a surreal design comically undercut with unique recipe in a bracketed aside, one of those voiced adjuncts that breaks from traditional poetry to make it not seem like poetry at all. The ad lib Bishop makes New Critics uneasy as the poetic form might not organically cohere anymore; but perhaps it is more organic than ever as we feel the whole poet embodies the poem. Then further on down, like Wallace Stevens, Bishop imagines drinking a *grog a l'americaine*; she lights the French-American cocktail on fire "with a kitchen match." Her domestic details established, for she had already stated that she'd "like to retire there and do *nothing* ... [except] look through binoculars, read boring books," like the poetic observer in "The Burglar of Babylon" and the narrator from her old 1938 autobiographical story, "In Prison." She has necessarily been building her proto-house ever since, even in her paintings such as *Olivia, Harris School, County Courthouse, Interior with Extension Cord, Interior with Calder Mobile* and *E. Bishop's Patented Slot Machine* that show the same formal lines with "a stove ... a chimney,/askew, but braces with wires,/and electricity, possibly/–at least, at the back another wire/limply leashes the whole affair." Much of Bishop's body electric would not be revealed until posthumous poems such as "Edgar Allan Poe & the Juke-Box," and "It is marvelous to wake up together." Meanwhile, in "The End of March," her crypto-dream-house for the poetic body is "perfect! But—impossible," as J. D. McClatchy noticed in an essay with that title.

"[O]f course the house was boarded up," as it was a dream prototype Bishop had been building for 40 years but could not inhabit (especially since this poem from *Geography III* in 1976 is published almost a decade after her dream-house architect, Lota de Macedo Soares, overdosed in Bishop's New York apartment). Back outside on the cold March beach of Duxbury, Massachusetts, "shadows" of stones "could have been teasing the lion sun," "a sun who'd walked the beach the last low tide" in iambic pentameter, "making those big, majestic paw-prints," now with five beats unevenly asserted by Bishop the observer of this day still predominantly ruled by Stevens' lion sun "who perhaps had batted a kite out of the sky to play with" (*PPL* 169). His aggressive swipe is the active agent of this mythopoetic picture with its line of string breakers, incidentally enacted by the retreat of Bishop's invisible kite (into blue imaginative oblivion). It is a dance of tribute to Stevens.

Note that this signature poem ends with its longest line, which extends rhythm, meter, and form excessively with prose, awkwardly ending with "with," a preposition of accompaniment in a lonely poem about human and poetic company that English students were taught not to end with. The aberrant preposition sounds unnatural, and together with the decidedly unreal mythic image of a lion batting a kite out of the sky, and an artichoke house, draws attention to superimposition on an everyday walk that's perfect but impossible.

* * *

Bishop's subtle subversions are quietly revolutionary yet pay homage to her master and her hosts. This may be one of her last giving up of the ghosts, along with "Crusoe in England" and other poems from *Geography III*. In her last poems such as "Santarém," "Pink Dog," and "Sonnet," she establishes complete abodes each unique with no ghosts. "[S]pontaneity occurs in a good *attack*, a rapid line, *tight* rhythm—" here she offers these qualities that she admired, in Auden's words, the "tension between natural speech and musical demands (which should be felt in every good lyric)" (Cook 124). In "Santarém," we have already observed natural and prosaic speech punctuated by intonations "*shush, shush, shush*" and rhetorical voices "*Graças a deus*" until Mr. Swan's rejoinder ironically elevates the gift to lyricize Bishop's musical demands. "Sonnet" is another example of traditional form renovated by Bishop's narrow lines that waveringly measure herself autobiographically until the final utterance, "gay!" (180). This word is both suddenly erratic and organically evolved as the poem moves from entrapment to liberation.

"Pink Dog" is perhaps most musical in fulfilling the criteria of "Grandmother's Glass Eye." Freakish by title, appearance, and treatment in Rio de Janeiro, the dog trots forward with steady gait in rhyming tercets. The poem's musicality on the page is complemented by its imagined participation in the sambas of Carnival, and by its sonic resonance with one of Brazil's best known songs of the time, "The Girl from Ipanema," as divulged by Lloyd Schwartz in conversation, and discussed by Maria Lúcia Milléo Martins in this book.

Bishop's every stanza engages with being startled: "Naked," "stare," "rabies/babies/scabies," "poor bitch," "beggars … in the tidal rivers" "bobbing in the ebbing sewage," legless with "life preservers," dog-paddling in a "*fantasía*," "a-/n eyesore" "in *máscara*" "degenerating" and "wonderful!" (178–179). "Remarkable," isn't it? The dog like the costumed revelers of Rio stands out constantly in each startling stanza that is part of a seemingly natural story, echoed by real news stories of unreal treatment of the poor that is shockingly real. The triple rhymes carry forward each stanza's narrative in unifications of sound that pull together the discordant elements. The precarious fate of the poor (floating amid sewage water in life preservers) is hardly a step up from the dog's sinking condition. And so the "solution is to wear a *fantasía*." The dressed-up costume and "*máscara*" that is part of it are presented in italics, a musical form of lettering to accompany the Carnival sambas because the dog "can't afford to be a-/n eyesore." See how the musical phrases are reflexively superimposed on the narrative? Bishop's images are artificial costumes (which are threatened by ruin) only to be urged to "Dress up and dance at Carnival!" The urgency of this call is felt in the physical action of the poem. In this movement, the poem's seemingly natural evolution is presented unnaturally in the makeup and dress-up apparel of dancing music.[3] (All of it a cover. A glass eye.)

Bishop's various late twentieth-century voices intone this new music in poetry. It is discordant and rhyming in "Pink Dog"; a sonnet stripped into a free halfness in "Sonnet"; ecstasy and insult in "Santarém"; perfectly impossible innovative house built from tradition in "The End of March"; true lies in "A Drunkard"; class critique that transcends identity borders in "Manuelzinho"; politeness ironized to criticize modern pace in "Manners." What else might she have done?

NOTES

1. In his "Hamlet" essay, T. S. Eliot writes: "The only way of expressing emotion in the form of art is by finding an 'objective correlative'; in other words, a set of objects, a situation, a chain of events which shall be the formula of that *particular* emotion .... Hamlet (the man) is dominated by an emotion which is inexpressible, because it is in *excess* of the facts as they appear" (*Selected Prose of T. S. Eliot*, 48).

2. Vidyan Ravinthiran writes a detailed analysis of the shifting identities, and Bishop's nuanced exploration of her response to class disjunctions in "'Manuelzinho,' Brazil and Identity Politics" in *Reading Elizabeth Bishop: An Edinburgh Companion*, edited by Jonathan Ellis. Ravinthiran begins the

essay by investigating the poem's oversimplified epigraph, "(Brazil. A friend of the writer is speaking.)" Vidyan also hears a lot of Bishop's voice: "That's to say, the sympathetic interval between Bishop and Lota is as relevant to 'Manuelzinho' as that which exists between the speaker and the man who lives on what she considers her land" (34–35). He thoroughly develops Bishop's unique presentation of what we now call identity politics while also attending to Brazil's contemporaneous political climate (33–47).

3. In "The Case of the Falling S: Elizabeth Bishop, Visual Poetry and the International Avant-Garde," Susan Rosenbaum demonstrates how Bishop's falling letters draw attention to rhyme and formal artifice: "we can read the truncation of the n as required by the rhyme: 'fantasía,' 'to be a-,' 'ever see a.' In the visibly awkward breakage of 'a-/n,' Bishop provides a visual, iconic analogy for 'eyesore.'" This is a "treatment of the desperation at once concealed and expressed by the costumes and dances of Carnival. The 'a-/n' provides a crucial crack in the poem's visual 'costume,' through which we glimpse the violent treatment that may await the naked dog and the necessity for the dog's disguise, simultaneously" (*Reading Elizabeth Bishop: An Edinburgh Companion* 185).

CHAPTER 9

Elizabeth Bishop and Brazilian Popular Music: From Anonymous Sambas to Contemporary Composers

Maria Lúcia Milléo Martins

Abstract Bishop's interest in Brazilian popular music is evident in many writings. In a letter to Lowell, she criticizes the carnival version in the movie *Orpheus*, manifesting her will to make "a good collection" of sambas in translation. She writes: "I suspect [sambas] are some of the last folk poetry to be made in the world." Besides the "anonymous four sambas" included in *Complete Poems*, Bishop translated a selection of well-known Brazilian composers. This unpublished repertoire was meant for a talk on Brazilian popular music at Bristol Community College in 1977, with poet Ricardo Sternberg on guitar. Considering Bishop's translations from the anonymous sambas to contemporary composers, this study discusses her critical views, cultural and political implications and resonances of Brazilian popular culture in her poetry.

Keywords Elizabeth Bishop • Brazilian popular music • Translation

M. L. M. Martins (✉)
Universidade Federal de Santa Catarina, Florianópolis, Brazil

© The Author(s) 2019
A. Cleghorn (ed.), *Elizabeth Bishop and the Music of Literature*,
Palgrave Studies in Music and Literature,
https://doi.org/10.1007/978-3-030-33180-1_9

Elizabeth Bishop's relation with Brazilian popular music is evident in many writings and results from a larger interest in different expressions of popular culture. In the section titled "Graceful and Popular Skills"[1] in the *Brazil* book, Bishop details various forms of folk art: craft, festivals and music, particularly the tradition of *cordel* and samba. First, she contextualizes the social conditions of poor people on the coast and the interior who produce this kind of art. She then explains their plurality as resultant from a mixture of different cultures, from the time of colonization, Portuguese, Moors, Native people and African slaves and, later, immigrants from other origins. Her appreciation of *cordel,* a poetic oral tradition of the Northeast, has resonance in her own work, in translations and in her poem "The Burglar of Babylon." Even more evident, her interest in samba and carnival constantly appear in different writings. Besides the anonymous sambas included in her *Complete Poems,* Bishop has translated a selection of well-known Brazilian composers. This unpublished repertoire was meant for a talk on Brazilian popular music at Bristol Community College in 1977, with poet Ricardo Sternberg on guitar. From *cordel* and samba to contemporary compositions, this study offers a contextual reading of Bishop's relation with Brazilian popular music, considering her critical views, translations and resonances in her own art.

Cordel tradition evokes the origins of poetry itself in its intimate relation with music. As Bishop comments in the *Brazil* book, this kind of poetry is improvised and sung by *cantadores* (singers) in their wanderings, accompanied by guitars or violins. Besides the rigorous metrics and challenge in poetic competitions, Bishop notes how this art used to incorporate the latest news, such as the death of President Getúlio Vargas, Yuri Gagarin's flight and President Jânio Quadros's resignation (86–87). *Cordel*'s tradition is present in Bishop's translation of João Cabral de Melo Neto's "Life and Death of a Severino" and in unfinished translations of folk songs.

Cabral's poem sings the saga of Severino, a Northeastern wanderer escaping the harshness of drought:

> We are many Severinos
> and our destiny's the same:
> to soften up these stones
> by sweating over them,
> to try to bring to life
> a dead and deader land,
> to try to wrest a farm
> out of burnt-over land.[2]

After surviving the fragility of life in this land, Severino tells about the drama of displacement: "I'll be the Severino/you'll now see emigrate" (63–64). Significantly, Bishop's poem "The Burglar of Babylon" begins with a depiction of the continuity of this history of migration to Rio:

On the fair green hills of Rio
    There grows a fearful stain:
The poor who come to Rio
    And can't go home again.

On the hills a million people,
    A million sparrows, nest,
Like a confused migration
    -That's had to light and rest. (*PPL* 90)

Bishop's foreword to the 1968 publication of the poem identifies "the poor who come to Rio" with these migrants from the Northeast, the *retirantes*. Another correspondence between the two poems is singing an individual drama representative of many. But most important, the two poets choose the lyrical ballad resembling *cordel* to approach the poetic language of popular culture. Reading some lines of the two poems aloud is enough to perceive the musicality, rhythm and rhyme, evoking *cordel* poetry.

Bishop's interest in this tradition is also present in her unfinished translations of a famous *cantador*, Anselmo Vieira de Souza, and other folk songs.[3] Bishop chooses a segment of Vieira de Souza's well-known *louvações* (songs in praise of who is hearing). In this case, the *cantador* praises a woman to the husband, saying in the initial lines that he will praise the wife "from head to heel." He boldly does this in a play of intimacy and admiration. The irony comes at the end with the risks of bulging with this wife. Unfortunately, there are only a few lines of Bishop's attempt to translate the poem.

Among Bishop's unfinished translations of folk songs, there is yet another one about the dramatic need of drinking, starting with the lines: "If I don't drink, I'd get dry/and dry I cannot sing." The simple language, wit and humor in these songs were certainly attractive to Bishop.

Bishop's interest in samba is a longer story, and usually appears related to carnival. In a letter to Robert Lowell in the 1960s, she criticizes the carnival version and sambas in the movie *Orpheus*:

The *Orpheus* music is pretty fakey, too—only one true samba—and the words, being written by a *real* poet, are bad—they lack that surprise, the misused words, the big words, etc., that sambas always have. One of my favorites has a refrain; "Respect the ambient!" And one about how Woman drags down Man—with all his "beauty and nobility."[4]

Bishop then manifests her intent to make "a good collection" of sambas in translation. In conclusion, she writes: "I suspect [sambas] are some of the last folk poetry to be made in the world."

The first collection of Bishop's translations of samba appeared in an essay titled "On the Railroad Named Delight," in the *New York Times*, on the occasion of Rio's 400th anniversary in 1965. Years later, these translations were incorporated in her *Complete Poems* with a brief introduction. To contextualize her choice, she says that, having appeared a year after the rightist revolution, this sampling "comments on, or pokes fun at power failures, government turnovers, and the hopelessly bad urban train" (*Poems* 251). Regina Przybycien comments that the content of these lyrics interested Bishop especially as examples of "the creative capacity of people in satirizing or poetizing their serious social and political problems. As in jokes, what attracted her most in sambas was humor, mockery" (58).[5] Marcos Napolitano contextualizes this feature of samba, explaining that the vitalizing presence of "the hill samba" and its mythical composers promoted a renewal of the genre. He says that if, since the 1930s, samba "meant Brazil," then in the 1950s a kind of "critical samba" asserted itself as a way of depicting the country's fragilities and contradictions (67). This "critical samba" survived the iron years of the military dictatorship in the 1960s, mastering the art of irony and satire. Bishop's selection of sambas illustrates this.[6]

The first samba, composed by Victor Simon and Fernando Martins, plays with *cariocas'* self-irony: "Rio de Janeiro,/My joy and my delight!/By day I have no water,/By night I have no light" (*PPL* 300). The title, "Firefly" ("Vagalume"), is taken from the last stanza where the poet's proposed solution is going to "the bush" looking for a firefly to give light to his "castle" (*cható*). With no use of subtlety, the second samba directly criticizes the rightist revolution—"Kick him out of office!/He's a greedy boy!/I've nothing to investigate,/What I want is joy!" The last lines, absent in Bishop's translation, make a reference to people fleeing to Uruguay and Spain in forced exile. Composed by Paquito, Romeu Gentil and Antônio Moreira da Silva, this samba surprisingly escaped censorship at the time. The third samba, by Wilson Batista and Jorge de Castro, audaciously addresses the then President Castelo Branco as "Illustrious Marshál," to "consider" the problem of urban transportation, telling him of the saga of suburbs. In a note, Bishop explains the references to "Leblon" and "Delight" (*"Encantado"*), "opposite ends of the city: the first, rich; the second, working class." The last samba, by Fernando Roberto, José Garcia and Jorge Martins, makes use of an old tradition in sambas of humorously depicting love dramas, inherited from the blues. Ingeniously naïve, the lines depict the poet begging the *mulata* to take him back: "You're the joker/In my pack,/The prune in my pudding,/Pepper in my pie,/My package of peanuts,/The moon in my sky." Although brief, the repertoire is representative not only of best-known sambas but of Brazil's social and political tensions at the time.

In Bishop's text "On the Railroad Named Delight," she regrets the deterioration of samba because of commercialism, television and radio. She writes:

> Ironically, what may prove to be the real kiss of death to the spontaneity of the samba is that the young rich, after years of devotion to North American jazz, have discovered it. A few years ago only the very few Brazilians, mostly intellectuals who cared for their own folk-culture took the samba seriously, or went to the rehearsals of the big schools up on the *morros*, the hills. (*PPL* 445)

Bishop then tells how this scenario changed with crowds of young people attending the rehearsals. Also, she criticizes the new songs, "far removed from the old samba spirit."

Bishop's interest in samba is not restricted to lyrics and music but extensive to the history and experience of samba. An unpublished text, possibly meant for *Black Beans and Diamonds* (the book on Brazil she could not finish), tells a sad carnival story, the death of a well-known *sambista*, Nair Pequena.[7] Bishop narrates the episode of her death on the avenue during the parade of her samba school, *Mangueira*. The text details how the school continued the parade in slow pace, silently, only with the sound of the *surdo* marking the step, and people's reactions. Voices of other *sambistas* and musicians join the narrative to tell the history of Nair Pequena and *Mangueira*. All agree that she died the way she wanted, dancing on the avenue. What stands out in Bishop's account is not so much the detailing of the death and rituals that followed, but empathy and admiration for the human bonds of samba. As Carmen Oliveira notes, Bishop "loved and respected samba and *sambistas*. She used to go frequently to *Zicartola*, the restaurant and show house of Cartola and [his wife], Dona Zica, and had a collection of records by Noel Rosa" (102). All these names have become important references in the history of samba.

Comments on carnival repeatedly appear in Bishop's writings. In a letter to Marianne Moore, she describes in detail the parade she attended in the company of Lota. She writes:

> The best ones are superb—several hundred Negroes dressed in silk and satins—white wigs and the styles of Louis XV are much favored, or the early colonial period here—with wonderful bands. [...] The crowd, and the outskirts of the crowd, are nice too—exhausted people in all sorts of costumes sitting along the curbs or stretched out on the grass.[8]

Although the aesthetic spectacle of carnival is the focus of Bishop's attention, she is sensitive to the experience of carnival on the margin of the parade. Right after this reference to the "exhausted" revelers on the streets, she describes a brief interaction with a couple and a tiny boy wearing a *fantasia*: "[W]hen Lota told him he was 'pretty' he smiled and then kissed our hands, in a gallant way." Years later, in a letter to James Merrill, she would regret missing Carnival for being away from Rio: "Sunday night was the 'samba schools,' the night I always attend, staying up all night and driving back to Petrópolis at dawn. Here I played a few samba *discos* I brought with me and samba-ed about all by myself."[9] The two comments demonstrate how Bishop's relation with carnival evolves from the position of mere observer to the one of reveler, yet alone and nostalgic.

Significantly in "Pink Dog," Bishop's last reference to carnival not only reiterates admiration but reveals recognition of its unique features.

> They say that Carnival's degenerating
> —radios, Americans, or something,
> have ruined it completely. They're just talking.
>
> Carnival is always wonderful!
> A depilated dog would not look well.
> Dress up! Dress up and dance at Carnival! (*PPL* 179)

Although carnival's degeneration may be attributed here to evils of commercialism, in the *Brazil* book, Bishop's criticism is more detailed. She says that radios destroy the "spontaneity" of carnival, promoting commercial songwriters and exhausting the songs long before the official dates. Although, by inference, "Americans" stand for tourists' damages, the target of Bishop's criticism is more precisely the American movie industry, responsible at the time for turning carnival into a "cinematic nightmare" (87–88). The final urge for the pink dog to "dress up and dance" enacts the spectacle of risk implied in the very soul of carnival, the daring humor in the face of hopeless situations. The surprising tone of bravado in the whole poem assimilates this.

While Bishop's interest in samba is recurrent in various writings, other rhythms of Brazilian popular music do not gain much of her attention. This is the case of *choro* and *bossa nova*. In the *Brazil* book, when discussing Brazilian sophisticated music, Bishop mentions the composer Villa-Lobos referring to his use of Portuguese, African, indigenous, folk and popular musical tradition. She then mentions his *Bachianas Brasileiras* and *choros*, frequently presented abroad. Originated from a combination of *lundu*, an African rhythm, with European musical genres *choros* circulated in Rio from the turn of the century, reaching popularity in the 1920s with Villa-Lobos and other composers. In the 1950s and 1960s, *choro* lost ground to *bossa nova*. Perhaps this explains why *choro* is absent in Bishop's references to Brazilian popular music. Although more familiar to Bishop, *bossa nova* appears only in brief references to songs like "Girl from Ipanema" (by Antonio Carlos Jobim and Vinicius de Moraes). As Ashley Brown puts it, Bishop "sort of liked bossa nova, but she preferred the old-fashioned thing, the samba" (*Remembering Elizabeth Bishop* 191). Brown then tells of his experience with Bishop in nightclubs in an old-fashioned quarter in Rio, where "everybody talked to everybody else and listened to the music," concluding that she had "a very real feeling for Brazilian popular culture."

Bishop's perception of Brazil as a musical country is also manifested in subtle details in her poetry. As Carmen Oliveira notes in "The Burglar of Babylon," the poet brings to the top of the hill "the remote modulations of the peanut vendor's whistle, and the umbrella seller's watchman's rattle" (101). Oliveira also mentions the depiction of the "childish *puta*" dancing "*chá-chá*" in the poem "Going to the Bakery." There are yet two references in the *Brazil* book that reveal Bishop's sensitivity to music in folk culture. When discussing the art of lacing, she mentions a folk song,

"Lace Maker" ("Mulher Rendeira"), related to the story of *Lampião*, a famous bandit in the Northeast. Bishop explains that his followers used to sing "Lace Maker" during horseback riding and translates its initial lines: "Oh, lacemaker!/Teach me to make lace/And I'll teach you how to love" (85). The other reference to folk music appears related to the celebration of "Beat my ox" ("Bumba-meu-boi") in the North and Northeast. When detailing the steps of the performance on the ox's life, death and resurrection, Bishop points out the importance of music open to improvisation.

As with relics that Bishop takes from Brazil to her apartment in Boston, objects of art, flavors (coffee, beans) and the best of Brazilian music remain with her. A talk on Brazilian poetry and music at Bristol Community College in 1977 confirms this. Bishop comments on her plans for this talk in an interview with Beatriz Schiller.[10] After a brief introduction to Sternberg, a Brazilian friend, Harvard student and poet, Bishop says: "In May we are going to do a program at a school near New Bedford, where the population is nearly all Portuguese. Ricardo plays the guitar. We are going to read and sing Brazilian poetry, in the original and in English translation." The selected repertoire includes Bishop's translations of seven songs by Brazilian composers: "The Yellow Ribbon," by Noel Rosa; "Conversation in the *Botequim*," by Noel Rosa and Vadico; "*A Banda*," by Chico Buarque de Hollanda; "Happiness," by Antonio Carlos Jobim and Vinicius de Moraes; "The Duck," by Jaime Silva and Neuza Teixeira; "Doralice," by Dorival Caymmi and Antonio Almeida; and "The Day I Went Away," by Caetano Veloso. In poetry, Bishop chooses her own translations of Carlos Drummond de Andrade and Vinicius de Moraes.[11]

In the brief introduction to the songs, Bishop informs that the first old samba by Noel Rosa, "Yellow Ribbon," is known to everyone, and the second, "Conversation of *Botequim*" (café or little bar) is an example of the composer's ability to "make a samba out of almost anything." An icon in the history of samba, "Yellow Ribbon" is a nostalgic foreshadowing of death but also a celebration of samba and eroticism. Instead of weeping and candles, the persona wants the cry of "flutes, guitars and *cavaquinhos*," and the *mulata* tap-dancing on his coffin. Bishop's collection of records by Noel Rosa certainly accounts for the appeal of both music and sagacity of lyrics.

"*A Banda*," by Buarque de Hollanda that Bishop recognizes as a "great hit" reviving old band-playing in Brazil, begins with an ordinary scene depicting somebody who is "doing nothing" and is invited to see "the band go by." Oliveira notes that, in the typed original of the song, Bishop makes a single note in English next to the expression *"estava à toa na vida,"* in her tiny handwriting: "I was doing nothing." Oliveira says that this is relevant and argues that Bishop's puritan background and Lota's pragmatic nature led the poet to confront the idea of having to "produce": "'Stop being lazy, go work, Cookie,' Lota's voice commanded while Bishop contemplated Manuelzinho and the donkey *Formoso*, 'just standing, staring/off into fog and space'" (102). Oliveira's observation also applies to Bishop's attraction to the slow pace of the provincial life in Ouro Preto, resembling Nova Scotia. In a letter to Mariette Charlton, she mentions the lines "What is this world, if full of care/We have no time to stop and stare...?"[12] to explain Ouro Preto's favorite sport: "window-leaning." Her poem on the town is evidence for her own practice. "*A Banda*" brings this provincial atmosphere in its cast of characters who see the town suddenly brightened as the band goes by. At the end, the band is gone and life returns to its routine. As for the music, Buarque de Hollanda revives the old rhythms of *marchinhas carnavalescas*, carnival songs that preceded the school sambas.

"Happiness," by Vinicius and Jobim, was another hit at the time. Bishop's brief note on Vinicius reiterates her comment in an interview to George Starbuck: "He was a very good poet, a serious one, somewhat Eliot-ish. He still is, but now he writes mostly popular songs, very good ones—'Girl from Ipanema,' for example."[13] There is no mention of Jobim in her note. As for the song "Happiness," it was initially composed as soundtrack for the film *Black Orpheus*. The chorus—"Sorrow has no end,/ but happiness, yes"—sustains a series of images illustrating the fragility of happiness. One of them refers to the "big illusion of Carnival," poor people who work all year long for "a moment's dream," and "everything is finished by Ash Wednesday." According to the program, before the song, Bishop would read her translation of Vinicius's "Sonnet of Intimacy." Bishop's friendship with Vinicius started by the time her old house in Ouro Preto was being restored. The two stayed at Pouso do Chico Rei, a small inn, where they spent long hours talking and drinking. At times, Vinicius would play his guitar and sing, and there are stories of the two poets singing together on the streets of Ouro Preto late at night.

A single line of introduction to the "The Duck," by Silva and Teixeira, and "Doralice," by Caymmi and Almeida, reads: "Two silly songs." The first plays with the impersonation of animals (duck, mallard, goose, swan) that join in a quartet of samba. The content of the lyrics may be silly, but the musical effect of words and the melodic line have a good level of sophistication. This was certainly a challenge for Bishop as translator. Recorded by many musicians, "The Duck" gained a unique interpretation in in the voice of João Gilberto, a famous singer of *bossa nova*. Also recorded by João Gilberto, "Doralice" (the beloved's name) is a lament for being caught up in a love trap. If there is something silly about the song, it applies to the persona playing the role of a clumsy lover. As with the samba begging the mulata to come back, the naïve lines evoke the tradition of love dramas from blues to samba.

The last song, "The Day I Went Away," by Veloso, has no introduction. It is part of the movement *Tropicália* in the late 1960s that opposed traditional or nationalistic trends, trying to universalize Brazilian musical language. To achieve this, *tropicalistas* incorporated elements of world culture, such as rock, psychedelia and electric guitar. In this sense, among all the songs in the selection, this is the most innovative. The theme of the song is leaving behind the paternal house to move to the capital, emblematic of *Tropicália*'s sense of liberation and adventure. The inclusion of more recent compositions and young composers like Veloso and Buarque de Hollanda in this selection shows that Bishop continued to update her collection of Brazilian popular music.

In "Some Memories of Elizabeth Bishop," Sternberg says that the talk at Bristol College was Bishop's idea. In a letter to his parents, she explains the plan: "We thought he could read in Portuguese, I could read translations, and then he could also play the guitar and sing. ... This won't pay much but I think it should be fun."[14] Sternberg says that, initially, they spoke about Brazilian modernist poetry and modern songwriting. He then explains: "I read in the original Portuguese a few of the poems in Elizabeth's anthology and she followed with the translations. I sang a few songs; she read translations of the lyrics" (36). Because the audience was not totally academic, Sternberg remembers Bishop as quite relaxed and enjoying the event.

Bishop's long story with Brazilian music reveals a genuine interest, a discreet passion. Her many writings on samba and her own translations along two decades are good evidence for this. Also relevant is the presence of *cordel* tradition in "The Burglar of Babylon." Not limited to specific musical genres, Bishop's poetic sensibility extended to a subtler perception of musicality around her. Besides the examples already mentioned, there is the memory of Santarém in precise notes of movement and silence—all variations of the rivers' musical stave, the only sounds in golden sands ("creaks and *shush, shush, shush*"), and the ship's final whistle.

In a more reserved way, musical Brazil also keeps on pulsing in Bishop's poem "Song for the Rainy Season," "the brook [singing] loud/from a rib cage/of giant fern." Small waterfalls, owl, frogs, all in this very private orchestra have accompanied the poet for long years. May these few notes of intimacy and coziness close here the repertoire of so many sounds of Brazil that Bishop has generously welcomed in her writings.

NOTES

1. In Bishop's drafts, the original title of this section is "The Unselfconscious Arts."
2. This excerpt is from section I: "The 'retirante' explains to the reader who he is and what he does," "The Death and Life of a Severino," *An Anthology of Twentieth-Century Brazilian Poetry*, 126.
3. Bishop's drafts with originals and unfinished translations belong to "Elizabeth Bishop Collection," Vassar College Library.
4. Bishop's letter to Lowell, April 22, 1960, *One Art*, 381–382.
5. I translate here this and other citations in Portuguese, keeping the original references.
6. This selection is kept in the new edition of Bishop's *Poems* and in *Elizabeth Bishop: Poems, Prose and Letters*.
7. "Elizabeth Bishop Collection," Vassar College Library.
8. Bishop's letter to Moore, February 23, 1958, *One Art*, 356.
9. Bishop's letter to Merrill, February 22, 1966, *One Art*, 445.
10. Jornal do Brasil, May 8, 1977, reprinted in *Conversations with Elizabeth Bishop*, 79.
11. Bishop's draft with translations and notes belongs to "Elizabeth Bishop Collection," Vassar College.
12. Bishop's letter to Charlton, July 24, 1969, "Elizabeth Bishop Collection," Houghton Library, Harvard University.
13. Reprinted in *Conversations with Elizabeth Bishop*, 96.
14. Bishop's letter, April 16, 1976, cited in Sternberg's essay, 35.

CHAPTER 10

'In Need of Music': Musical Settings of Elizabeth Bishop

Lloyd Schwartz

Abstract Beginning in 1957, poems of Elizabeth Bishop have been set to music by four Pulitzer Prize-winning composers and a popular Brazilian singer and songwriter. This chapter will discuss the way each of these composers—Ned Rorem, Elliott Carter, John Harbison, Yehudi Wyner, and Luciana Souza—approached her writing. Special emphasis will be given to the two major song cycles (Carter and Harbison), which have been recorded and widely performed.

Keywords Musical settings • Composers • Elliott Carter • John Harbison • Song cycles

In the interview that Ned Rorem gave to the editors of *Remembering Elizabeth Bishop*, the composer of the very first musical settings of her poems put his finger on a paradox. Bishop, he says, "was one of those poets who are interested in the fact that you might set their work to music

L. Schwartz (✉)
University of Massachusetts, Boston, MA, USA

© The Author(s) 2019
A. Cleghorn (ed.), *Elizabeth Bishop and the Music of Literature*,
Palgrave Studies in Music and Literature,
https://doi.org/10.1007/978-3-030-33180-1_10

and are sort of flattered, but are inevitably disappointed. But how can they help but be? They heard their own music when they wrote it" (159).

Rorem was right. Hearing his two settings, in 1957, she questioned whether they were in the right key, the right tempo, and whether they should be sung by a man rather than a woman. His music just wasn't "the music she had in her mind."

When in 1953 Bishop's musician friends Arthur Gold and Robert Fizdale first suggested Bishop to Rorem, he initially found her poems too "prosey." The composer Virgil Thomson read him "Visits to St. Elizabeths" just after it appeared in *Partisan Review*. But he hadn't thought it was right for a musical setting. Then he changed his mind. He ended up setting (or "planned to" set) seven of her poems, though only two of them were eventually published: "Visits to St. Elizabeths" and "Conversation," the first of her sequence "Four Poems" (from *A Cold Spring*), a cryptic love poem that ends "until a name/and all its connotation are the same" (*PPL* 58). He admits that some of these settings were intended "to express my broken heart, and you can't do that" (*Remembering Elizabeth Bishop* 159).

Rorem calls "Visits to St. Elizabeths (Bedlam)" a "virtuoso" piece—very fast, even manic. Regina Sarfaty, the mezzo-soprano who made the first recording, had trouble spitting out all the words. He recalls that at the premiere Patricia Neway (best remembered as the mother superior who introduced the world to "Climb Every Mountain" in *The Sound of Music*) wore her long hair in a bun, then began taking out her hairpins "one by one ... so that by the end of the song she looked like a gibbering idiot. The audience loved it."

The structure of the poem is in incremental verses, like "The House That Jack Built." In Rorem's setting, the word "Bedlam," repeated at the end of each verse, slips unexpectedly into the "wrong" key. But it's practically the only word Rorem sets for its meaning. There's a lost opportunity to "point" Bishop's words. "The Jew in the newspaper hat" and a loopy sailor are as anonymous as the "tragic," "honored," "brave," "cranky," "cruel," "busy," "tedious," and "wretched" poet (Ezra Pound), all inmates at St. Elizabeths. Rorem's musical hysteria undercuts the essential—and ever-increasing—melancholy of Bishop's words.

Rorem's setting of "Conversation" also has its share of anonymity, of a mid-twentieth-century academic sort. And while it's true that Bishop didn't comprehend Elliott Carter's more personal and adventurous settings nearly two decades later, the less-challenging Rorem settings remain a disappointment, and not only to Bishop herself.

Carter is one of our great readers of poetry, especially American poetry. As an undergraduate, he was, after all, an English major. His early, rebellious love of modernism wasn't limited to music. The poets he chose to set—to *read*—included Emily Dickinson and Walt Whitman, Robert Frost, and such diversely heroic modernist figures as Hart Crane, Allen Tate, John Ashbery, Robert Lowell, Wallace Stevens—and Bishop.

These choices don't merely reflect Carter's taste—they express central aspects of his own complex character. Frost's sly and crusty humor wells up from a tragic sense of isolation—the sublime indifference of nature mirroring our detachment from one another. Carter the innovator might well identify with Hart Crane's desire to create a new and complex lyric rhetoric, or with the seriousness underlying the glitter of Ashbery's slippery, "surfacey" aesthetic. Lowell, like Carter, remains more clearly than ever the spiritual and psychological voice of our time, an artist who has moved between probing self-analysis and large-scaled public utterance, between an intricate and gorgeous poetic density and the poignant directness of conversation. And Bishop's reticence and elusiveness, like Carter's, are mixed with a profound—and profoundly American—sensibleness and forthrightness, at their most "mercurial" (one of Carter's favorite words).

Bishop admired writers who could re-create the "mind thinking." Carter's remarkable settings share this quality of looking and reaching outward into the life of the world, but also retreating deeply into the most secret self, speaking the language of inward isolation that in music no twentieth-century American composer has expressed more deeply. Carter had given up vocal writing for nearly a quarter of a century; then when he returned to setting poetry, in 1975, the poet was Bishop.

A Mirror on Which to Dwell is his cycle of six Bishop poems (the title comes from Bishop's poem "Insomnia"). Though some of the music is breathtakingly melodic, the center of these settings is in the interaction between voice and accompaniment, the continually evolving contexts for the voice. This does not mean that the voice is merely another instrument of the orchestra, or even the "main" instrument. The voice carries the human experience. Carter doesn't always (or often) set a text the way anyone might expect it to be set (certainly not the way Bishop expected). But for him the words are crucial, and the settings always illuminate the words. In his first draft of "Anaphora," his marks over the words are not musical notes but an attempt to show the inflections of reading the poem aloud. The score to "Anaphora" reads: "Although the voice participates in the ensemble, its line with the indicated dynamic shadings must clearly predominate throughout. Instrumental dynamics should be adjusted, wherever necessary, to produce this result."

Bishop is the master of Keatsian "negative capability"—the art of being content to remain in "uncertainties, mysteries, doubts." The poems Carter chose for *A Mirror on Which to Dwell* were all written between 1945 and 1962, before the last phase of her writing in which she finally incorporated explicitly autobiographical details. The three "personal" love poems that punctuate this cycle ("Argument," "Insomnia," "O Breath") speak a general, abstract but dazzlingly imagistic language about the ambivalent nature of relationships: the "I" and the "You" are more generic than individual, even though the "You" has a startlingly specific "nine black hairs/four around one five the other nipple." These are Modern Lovers, engaged more in seeking reconciliation than happiness:

> something that maybe I could bargain with
> and make a separate peace beneath
> within if never with. (*PPL* 60)

These poems of physical and psychological separation (i.e., "love" poems) alternate with poems that depict the ways of the external world: natural, social, and political. Carter told me that his choices were "considerations about nature, love, and isolation." "Anaphora" (which literally means "a carrying back") is the rhetorical repetition of the first word in a series of phrases (as in "I came, I saw, I conquered"), the poem's major literary device as well as its subject. The poem is about repetitions, the daily recycling of splendor ("such white-gold skies our eyes/first open on"), deterioration ("mortal/mortal fatigue"), and rejuvenation ("endless/endless assent"). "Each day with so much ceremony/begins," and then ends with "the beggar in the park" (the sun? the poet?—for Carter, "a figure symbolizing Day") "who, weary, without lamp or book/prepares stupendous studies."

"Anaphora" was the last poem in Bishop's first book, a dreamlike, *Finnegans Wake*-ish summing up of life cycles, melancholy yet consoling. Carter turns it into a formal opening "ceremony" of annunciation, a public concert—birds, church bells, factory whistles—that Carter reproduces in a shimmering cacophony of wind trio, strings, piano, and vibraphone that the narrative voice has to elbow through.

The ritual repetitions of "Anaphora" lead Carter to the agitated (Allegro agitato) repetitions of "Argument," the "gentle battleground" of two lovers kept apart by "Days and Distances"—the "facts" of separation that "argue, argue, argue with me/endlessly" (the arguing piquantly rendered by four angry bongo drums). Repetitions continue in "Sandpiper," the "poor bird" looking "for something, something, something" among the "millions of grains" of sand, "preoccupied," "finical, awkward,/in a state of controlled panic," "obsessed."

The sandpiper is, of course, the alter ego of the poet, one of Bishop's most poignant and witty (though veiled) images of herself—an idea Carter picks up on by choosing for the obbligato his own instrument, the oboe, to represent this "student of Blake," pecking away, trying to find the world in a grain of sand. "The world," he discovers in the most expansive, soaring legato in the entire cycle, "is a mist." It is also, paradoxically, both "minute and vast"—and can even be at moments, for the artist, "clear."

The juxtaposition of "Sandpiper" and "Insomnia" implies a parallel between the artist's daylight preoccupations and the inverted world (Bishop writes "world inverted"), the looking glass in which his "night fantasies" (the title of one of his major piano works) play themselves out. Here, "left is always right," "the shadows are really the body," and the dream of love is actually fulfilled.

The setting of this poem has Carter's sparest musical surface: piccolo, violin, viola, and marimba at its glassiest. While the next poem, "View of the Capitol from the Library of Congress" (where Bishop was Consultant in Poetry, 1949–1950), is the most public and satiric in the cycle and has the densest surface. It's practically a homage to Ives, Carter's early and most important mentor. It's another poem with music within it. "Snatches" of the Air Force Band playing a march can be heard in the distance (*Alla marcia—quasi da lontano*), but in this Ivesian sound montage "the music doesn't quite come through." The Cold War gets in the way of art. Puns abound, as the tone of the poem gets more hyperbolically mock-heroic ("The gathered brasses want to go/*boom—boom*") and the music gets both funnier and grimmer—the last two words "intensely whispered," the accompanying strings seem to be playing "angrily."

The sixth and last poem in the cycle is "O Breath"—one of Bishop's most painfully moving and intimate love poems, her ultimate image of personal isolation (between lovers, between human beings). It's remarkably revealing that Carter should have chosen to end the series here. What could be more crucial to a musician or a singer than breath itself? Carter honors Bishop's spaces for breath midway through each line. (He asks the soprano to sing "as if out of breath"). He also captures her sense of indrawn intimacy (it's the quietest setting in the sequence—nothing louder than *p*). The soprano's fluttering roulades are an unsettling mixture of Viennese expressionism and Italian bel canto; desperate, breathless urgency; and phenomenal technical control. The poet and the composer are stoic, resigned; the personal and public conflicts they face remain unresolved, unresolvable.[1]

Bishop, as Rorem intuited, may have indeed wanted more of her poems set to music, but she lived to hear only Rorem's two settings and the Carter cycle, which the distinguished contemporary music group that commissioned it, Speculum Musicae, and the eloquent soprano Susan Davenny-Wyner, performed in her presence and in her honor at the Modern Language Association annual conference, in New York in 1976. She admired Carter (probably more than Rorem), but was bewildered, mystified by how different these settings were from her sense of her own poems. Never in her lifetime did she hear a setting of her poems that she completely approved of, much as she may have wanted to.

The next major song cycle based on her work didn't occur—and couldn't have occurred—until after her death (I'll explain below). The Pulitzer Prize and MacArthur Foundation grant-winning John Harbison has always been an inspired setter of great poetic texts—poems often exploring the shadowy ambiguities and uncertainties of emotional, spiritual, ethical, and even political questions, and the very nature and function of art itself. The span of his poetry selections is astonishing, including complete plays by Shakespeare (*A Winter's* Tale) and Yeats (*A Full Moon in March*) and, one of his masterpieces, his hour-long setting, in Italian, of Eugenio Montale's subtle and heartbreaking *Motetti*, for which Montale himself gave his rare approval.

Harbison's first Bishop settings appeared as part of his cycle *Flashes and Illuminations* (1991), a rangy "anthology" of poems that demonstrate the "momentary perception of the natural world or a human interaction that brings sudden insight" (Harbison's program note). This work included Bishop's two poems with French titles, "Chemin de Fer" and "Cirque d'Hiver."

Harbison has admitted that it took him a long time to get to (and *get*) Bishop. His breakthrough was encountering her early "Cirque d'Hiver," which is the most delicate and touching song in *Flashes and Illuminations*. In that poem, Bishop is watching with resigned awe—and identifying with (as a person and artist)—a little mechanical horse going through its mechanical paces, carrying ("bearing") on his back a dainty mechanical ballerina wearing a spray of artificial roses ("He is the more intelligent by far"). At the end of the poem (the flash of illumination!), Bishop directly confronts the toy horse:

Facing each other rather desperately—
his eye is like a star—
we stare and say, "Well, we have come this far." (*PPL* 24)

In its poignant elegance and grave, half-comic, Keatonesque humility, it's an archetypal poem for Harbison. And it opened the floodgates. His next Bishop project was, like Carter's Bishop setting, a six-poem cycle, *North and South* (1999/2001), composed for, and premiered by, the profound mezzo-soprano Lorraine Hunt Lieberson, and includes two poems Bishop never published during her lifetime. Harbison's first version was with piano accompaniment, and he revised it for chamber orchestra. This was soon followed by the impressive *Aria: Song for the Rainy Season* (2002). Harbison even began working on an opera based on Bishop's life (until the funding for this commission fell through).

North and South (eschewing the cheekier ampersand that Bishop used in the title of her first book) ranks among Harbison's most moving and complex musical sequences. It's in two parallel "books" of three poems each. And at least five of the poems have various explicit references to music. Each book begins with the blues: the first two of Bishop's four "Songs for a Colored Singer," which Harbison calls "Ballads for Billie"— partly because the second of these is in the intricate form of the ballad, and partly because Bishop had hoped someone would set them for Billie Holiday, which, in effect, is just what Harbison has done. These settings are the most overtly jazzy movements in all his "serious" music. The poems are both poignant and hilarious: "I'm going to go and take the bus/And find someone monogamous" (is there any other composer who could do the tetrasyllabic "monogamous" such musical justice?).

The parallel second songs in each book are both like short scherzos— one fast and one slow. "Late Air" (Book I) is about lovers stretched out on the dew-wet grass listening to love songs broadcast from a radio tower in Key West. The notes rise and fall disconnectedly up and down the scale as Bishop compares the lights of the towers to flashing phoenixes. Especially in the version with piano, the sweeping runs surrounding the opening phrase ("From a magician's midnight sleeve") are like the wave of a silk scarf. "Song" (Book II) is more ironic, since the actual "song" of the title is this little poem itself, which pictures a deserted end-of-summer harbor and the memory of a yacht once anchored there, "stepping and side-stepping like Fred Astaire," as Harbison's music, a lullaby, rocks nostalgically back and forth.

The last poems in each book are love poems that Bishop never published in her lifetime, but two of the most substantial and polished of her posthumously published poems. "Breakfast Song" (another musical title) is a contemporary *aubade*, which Harbison sets as a slow, lilting waltz:

> My love, my saving grace,
> your eyes are awfully blue.
> I kiss your funny face,
> your coffee-flavored mouth.
> Last night I slept with you.
> Today I love you so
> how can I bear to go
> (as soon I must, I know)
> to bed with ugly death
> in that cold, filthy place,
> to sleep there without you.... (*PPL* 256–257)

The poem is as autumnal as Shakespeare's Sonnet 73 ("That time of year thou may'st in me behold"), which is also about two lovers widely separated in age, the older facing death yet acknowledging that mortality, the inevitability that this love must soon have to end actually serves to make that love "more strong." For Bishop, her horror of being forced to "go ... to bed with ugly death," her fear of sleeping in that—she can't even bear to name it—"cold, filthy place ... without you,/without the easy breath/and nightlong, limblong warmth/I've grown accustomed to," is unbearable. The only comfort lies in living in the present moment itself, in the vitality and beauty of the beloved, her "saving grace," whose "eyes are awfully blue/early and instant blue." Harbison's slow waltz is the embodiment of the art (the "one art") that transcends death.

The last poem in Harbison's cycle, untitled and beginning "Dear, my compass/still points north," is the one song without an explicit musical allusion. For Bishop, "north" was both literal, a reference to the New England and Nova Scotia of her childhood that she sees with nostalgia from the point of view of her life in Brazil, and also the "north" of fairy tales ("where/flaxen-headed/younger sons/bring home the goose"). In Harbison's *North and South*, it's the one place, the mythic place, where these lovers, inevitably from opposite poles of the world and with polar opposite temperaments, might try but will probably fail to meet (as they fail to come together in "Insomnia" and "O Breath"). The words sail over Harbison's restless chaconne that grows increasingly urgent as the fairy tale becomes more ominous, violent, and sexual ("crab-apples/ripen to rubies,/cranberries/to drops of blood"). Suddenly, all movement stops, as the poem abruptly shifts gears and acknowledges its "real" subject matter, and ends, like so many of Harbison's pieces, with a quiet shrug of resigned acceptance:

> —Cold as it is, we'd
> go to bed, dear,
> early, but never
> to keep warm. (*PPL* 251)

Bishop's most ambitious and fully dramatized love poem is "Song for the Rainy Season" (from *Questions of Travel*), and in *Aria: Song for the Rainy Season*, which Harbison had intended for his Bishop opera, he precedes it with another, shorter love lyric Bishop abandoned in Brazil, "Close, close all night," which he sets as a kind of hymn (the combined winds sounding like an organ).

It's his prologue to what Harbison calls "a grand and subtle rendering of the sovereignty of nature and … a metaphor for the mutability and collapse of Bishop's relationship." Bishop had been living in Brazil with Lota de Macedo Soares, her new lover, and for the first time since her earliest childhood she had finally found a place she could call home, where she could *feel* at home. In Brazil, high in the mountains just north of Rio, in this season of mists ("rain-, rainbow-ridden") and mellow fruitfulness, all Nature is welcome in their loving house, an "open house"—open

> to the white dew
> and the milk-white sunrise
> kind to the eyes,
> to membership
> of silver fish, mouse,
> bookworms,
> big moths…. (*PPL* 82)

Harbison's music here is as delicate as raindrops and full of burbling brooks, shrill woodwind birdcalls, and animal squeals (including literally "horny" frogs). The house seems to be surrounded by universal lovemaking ("the fat frogs that,/shrilling for love,/clamber and mount"), far from neat but cause for celebration: "maculate, cherished,/rejoice!" The music gradually increases in urgency and climactic passion.

Then the key changes. Bishop is also aware that this joy, this celebration, can't last. That there is—always—a different season ("O difference that kills"), "without water," in which all this messy, juicy intimacy will eventually dry up and shrivel, that their neighboring mountain will be "no longer wearing/rainbows or rain"—the protecting privacy of the fog and the "forgiving air" soon "gone"—and the aria dwindles (with the tunelessly spoken word "shrivels") into a calmly accepting and evaporating postlude.

As Harbison acknowledges, Bishop loved popular music. She was a fan not only of Billie Holiday and Ella Fitzgerald but also of Donovan ("Mellow Yellow") and Chubby Checker ("The Twist"). One of her best friends in Brazil was the celebrated songwriter ("The Girl from Ipanema"), playwright (*Black Orpheus*), and poet Vinicius de Moraes. Two more recent groups of musical settings of Bishop poems have appeared in a more traditionally lyric or popular mode.

In a plan to celebrate the Bishop centennial in 2011, Canadian soprano Suzie LeBlanc, Nova Scotian composer Alasdair MacLean, and poet and Bishop scholar Sandra Barry teamed up to commission a series of songs from Canadian composers, which appeared on a CD in 2013 called *I am in need of music*, with LeBlanc accompanied by the Blue Engine String Quartet and the Elizabeth Bishop Players, a chamber orchestra under the direction of Dinuk Wijeratne.

MacLean's contribution is *Silken Water: The Elizabeth Bishop Suite*, the first movement of which is a short, purely instrumental, conventionally atmospheric selection for strings responding to Bishop's line from her poem "Cape Breton": "The silken water is weaving and weaving." This is followed by attractive, unthreatening orchestral settings of the same three posthumously published poems Harbison used in *North and South*, but here Bishop's verbal surprises seem unprobing and a little ironed out.

Perhaps the major addition to the Bishop repertoire on this disc is one of the two songs by John Plant (Canadian since 1968, but born in Yonkers), the ambitious 15-minute-long "Sunday, 4 A.M."—one of Bishop's oddest, most cryptic dream poems. Plant's setting not always observes Bishop's quatrains, so is as full of surprises as the poem itself, alternating between slashing strings and tickling pizzicatos, ending with lines hauntingly drawn out. Plant's other contribution, "Sandpiper," for piano and winds, is very different from Carter's, yet has a parallel sense of anxiety, especially in the crescendo on the poor obsessed bird "looking for something, something, something." The high voice and glittering piano capture Bishop's literally jewel-like conclusion:

The millions of grains are black, white, tan, and gray,
Mixed with quartz grains, rose and amethyst. (*PPL* 126)

Emily Doolittle's "A Short, Slow Life" brings another of Bishop's best posthumously published poems into the conversation. Doolittle plays inventively with timing, as is right for a poem dealing with time as a threat. Her pizzicato repetitions on the phrases "hid like white crumbs" and "fluff of gray willows" followed by languorous melismas leaves us both hypnotized and questioning.

LeBlanc's collection ends with four songs by Greek-Canadian composer Christos Hatzis. The early "Sonnet" ("I am in need of music") and "Anaphora" are lovely and lush old-fashioned lyrical outpourings, sentimental quasi-parlor songs with orchestra, neither one seriously contending with the words, although perhaps reflecting the dated inversions of the syntax in the earlier poem. My favorite Hatzis is "Insomnia," a bouncy and tuneful folk-like setting quite the opposite of Carter's glistening sophistication. Hatzis sets "The Unbeliever" as an off-kilter waltz, operetta-like, with an oddball horn obbligato. I can't quite figure out how this music connects to the poem, but the choices are interesting enough to keep me guessing. It ends—on the words "The spangled sea below wants me to fall,/It is hard as diamonds; it wants to destroy us all"—not with a bang but an actual whisper.

Bishop herself might have preferred what are stylistically the most popular and least "classical" settings of her poems. Israeli superstar David Broza recorded his gently consoling rock version of "One Art" (under the title "The Art of Losing") in 1994. Brazilian jazz singer and composer Luciana Souza's *The Poems of Elizabeth Bishop* CD (2000) includes the early "Sonnet" twice, and Souza is so inside the texts that she can toss off a word like "subaqueous" (her diction is impeccable) and make it convincingly unselfconscious and unpretentious. She sets (and sings) "Argument" as a melancholy torch song, the sincerity of her delivery the opposite of Carter's lovers' witty battlefield. The new contribution here is the posthumously published "Imber Nocturnus," a moody and atmospheric embodiment of Bishop's least known poem about lovers and rain.

It's surprising that what has become the most frequently set of Bishop's poems is not one of her best or most important poems. That early "Sonnet" beginning "I am in need of music" practically begs for (and maybe needs) a musical setting. Combing through YouTube, I stumbled across a version by American composer Ben Moore from 2001, which diva Deborah Voigt

included on an album of American songs, and an even prettier choral setting by the American choral composer David L. Brunner, which dates at
least from 2007. Dreamy and consoling, it's soothing in a perhaps overly
familiar choral style, with what might be the prettiest tune for any Bishop
poem (it reminds some people of "Beauty and the Beast").

But the most illuminating setting of "Sonnet" is its most recent musical incarnation, presented without much fanfare at the Tanglewood
Festival of Contemporary Music in 2015 as part of a "prelude" to a
Boston Symphony Orchestra concert. Yehudi Wyner's *Sonnet: In the
Arms of Sleep* is a miracle, the 86-year-old master's setting of a poem
Bishop wrote when she was a precocious 17 (having just heard a piano
recital by the legendary Myra Hess). It was the first of two poems she
titled "Sonnet" (the other was essentially her last poem, first published
shortly after her sudden death). The young poet, infatuated with the allit-
erative verse of Gerard Manly Hopkins, yearns for music to "flow/Over
my fretful, feeling, fingertips."

The poem begins "I am in need," and Wyner isolates and insistently
repeats young Bishop's opening phrase. These inspired repetitions change
the poem. As his own title (*In the Arms of Sleep*) suggests, he turns the
young poet's wish for future music into a retrospective gaze over a whole
life of *making* music: "Oh, for the healing. ... Of some song sung to rest
the tired dead"; "There is a magic" (achingly slow); "A spell of rest, and
quiet breath" [*PPL* 186]. In an act of deep imagination, Wyner transforms
the artifice of Bishop's youthful formality into something completely new
and personal—significantly more urgent and *felt* than the original poem.

The song was written for veteran new-music soprano and legendary
voice teacher Lucy Shelton, who was joined by two young mezzo-soprano
vocal fellows, who echoed what she was singing—everything further
amplified by the haunting harmonies of strings, winds, and harp. This new
work was the most moving in the entire Festival of Contemporary Music
and for me joins Carter and Harbison as a major addition to the slowly
growing catalog of musical settings of Bishop.

NOTE

1. A version of this section on Carter appeared in my essay "Elliott Carter and
   American Poetry," *Elliott Carter: The Vocal Works (1975–1981)*, Bridge
   Records, 1989.

WORKS CITED

Albright, Daniel, ed. *Modernism and Music: An Anthology of Sources*. Chicago University Press, 2004.

Ardoin, Paul, S. E. Gontaski, and Laci Mattison, eds. *Understanding Bergson, Understanding Modernism*. Bloomsbury, 2013.

Barnes, Jonathan. *Aristotle: A Very Brief Introduction*. Oxford University Press, 2000.

Baudelaire, Charles. *Oeuvres Complètes*, vol. 1. Gallimard, Bibliothèque de la Pléiade, 1975.

———. *Les Fleurs du Mal et Oeuvres Choisies*. Ed. Wallace Fowlie. New York: Dover Publications, 1992.

Benjamin, Walter. "The Translator's Task." Translated by Steven Rendall. *TTR: traduction, terminologie, rédaction* 10:2 (1997): 151–165; http://www.enl.auth.gr/staff/apostolou/the_Translator's_Task.pdf; accessed 25 Nov 2017.

Bidart, Frank. "On Elizabeth Bishop." *Elizabeth Bishop and Her Art*, eds. Lloyd Schwartz and Sybil P. Estess. University of Michigan Press, 1983: 214–216.

Bishop, Elizabeth. *One Art: Letters*. Ed. Robert Giroux. NY: Farrar, Straus and Giroux, 1994.

———. *Exchanging Hats: Elizabeth Bishop Paintings*. Ed. William Benton. Carcanet Press, 1997.

———. *Edgar Allan Poe & the Juke-Box: Uncollected Poems, Drafts, and Fragments*. Ed. Alice Quinn. NY: Farrar, Straus and Giroux, 2006.

———. *Poems, Prose, & Letters*. Eds. Robert Giroux and Lloyd Schwartz. New York: Library of America, 2008.

———. *Poems*. NY: Farrar, Straus and Giroux, 2011a.

© The Author(s) 2019
A. Cleghorn (ed.), *Elizabeth Bishop and the Music of Literature*,
Palgrave Studies in Music and Literature,
https://doi.org/10.1007/978-3-030-33180-1

————. *Prose*. Ed. Lloyd Schwartz. NY: Farrar, Straus and Giroux, 2011b.

————. *Elizabeth Bishop and The New Yorker: The Complete Correspondence*. Ed. Joelle Biele. Farrar, Straus and Giroux, 2011c.

————. *Elizabeth Bishop Collection*. Vassar College. Poughkeepsie, NY.

Bishop, Elizabeth, and Robert Lowell. *Words in Air: The Complete Correspondence Between Elizabeth Bishop and Robert Lowell*. Eds. Thomas Travisano with Saskia Hamilton. NY: Farrar, Straus and Giroux, 2008.

Bishop, Elizabeth, and The Editors of *Life*. *Brazil*. New York: Life World Library, Time Inc., 1962.

Bishop, Elizabeth, and Emanuel Brasil, eds. *An Anthology of Twentieth-Century Brazilian Poetry*. Hanover and London: Wesleyan University Press, 1972.

Boland, Eavan, and Mark Strand. *The Making of a Poem: A Norton Anthology of Poetic Forms*. Norton, 2001.

Boland, Eavan. Review of *On Elizabeth Bishop* by Colm Tóibín. *The Irish Times*, 24 April 2015. https://www.irishtimes.com/culture/books/eavan-boland-reviews-on-elizabeth-bishop-by-colm-t%C3%B3ib%C3%ADn-1.2146004; accessed April 24, 2019.

Brogan, T. V. F. "Sound." *The New Princeton Encyclopedia of Poetry and Poetics*, eds. Alex Preminger and T. V. F. Brogan. Princeton UP, 1993: 1172–1180.

Brown, Ashley. "An Interview with Elizabeth Bishop." *Elizabeth Bishop and Her Art*, eds. Lloyd Schwartz and Sybil P. Estess. University of Michigan Press, 1983: 289–302.

Broza, David. *Second Street*. November Records, 1994.

Brunner, David. "I am in need of music," Tennessee Tech University, 2010. https://www.youtube.com/watch?v=Dx-AoJFwApk&list=RDDx-AoJFwApk&index=1

Burt, Stephanie, and David Mikics. *The Art of the Sonnet*. Harvard UP, 2011.

Carter, Elliott. *The Vocal Works (1975–1981)*, Bridge Records, 1989.

————. *A Mirror on Which to Dwell*, Susan Davenny Wyner, Speculum Musicae, *Pierre Boulez: The Complete Columbia Album Collection*, Sony, 2016.

Cleghorn, Angus, and Jonathan Ellis. *The Cambridge Companion to Elizabeth Bishop*. Cambridge UP, 2014.

Cleghorn, Angus. "Bishop's Stevensian Architecture," unpublished conference paper. Elizabeth Bishop in Paris: Spaces of Translation and Translations of Space. University of Paris-Sorbonne, June 6–8, 2018.

Cook, Eleanor. *Elizabeth Bishop at Work*. Harvard UP, 2016.

Costello, Bonnie. *Elizabeth Bishop: Questions of Mastery*. Harvard UP, 1991.

————. "Elizabeth Bishop's Impersonal Personal." *American Literary History* 15:2 (2003): 334–366.

————. "Bishop and the Poetic Tradition." *The Cambridge Companion to Elizabeth Bishop*, eds. Angus Cleghorn and Jonathan Ellis. Cambridge UP, 2014.

de Souza, Luciana. *The Poems of Elizabeth Bishop and Other Songs*. Sunny Side, 2000.

Dolar, Mladen. *A Voice and Nothing More*. MIT Press, 2006.

Eliot, T. S. "The Music of Poetry," in *On Poetry and Poets*. Faber, 1957.

———. *Selected Prose of T.S. Eliot*. Ed. Frank Kermode. NY: Farrar, Straus and Giroux, 1975.

Ellis, Jonathan. *Reading Elizabeth Bishop: An Edinburgh Companion*. Edinburgh University Press, 2019.

Freer, Alexander. "Rhythm as Coping." *New Literary History* 46:3 (Summer 2015): 549–568.

Fountain, Gary, and Peter Brazeau, eds. *Remembering Elizabeth Bishop: An Oral Biography*. University of Massachusetts Press, 1996.

Frosch, Thomas. "Wordsworth's 'Beggars' and a Brief Instance of 'Writer's Block'." *Studies in Romanticism* 21:4 (1982): 619–636.

Harbison, John. *Chamber Music*, Lorraine Hunt Lieberson, The Chicago Chamber Musicians, Naxos, 2006.

Galassi, Johnathan. "The Illusion of Utter Transparency." *The New York Review of Books*, May 11, 2017: 26–28.

Ginsberg, Allen. *Collected Poems, 1947–1997*. HarperCollins Publishers, 2006.

Giroux, Robert, ed. *One Art: The Selected Letters*. Pimlico, 1996.

Goldensohn, Lorrie. "Bishop's Posthumous Publications." *The Cambridge Companion to Elizabeth Bishop*, eds. Angus Cleghorn and Jonathan Ellis. Cambridge UP, 2014.

Hammer, Langdon. "The New Elizabeth Bishop." *Yale Review* 82:1 (1994): 135–149.

Heaney, Seamus. *The Government of the Tongue: Selected Prose 1978–1987*. Farrar, Straus and Giroux, 1989.

Jarrell, Randall. *Poetry and the Age*. Expanded edition, UP of Florida, 2001.

———. "On *North & South*." *Elizabeth Bishop and Her Art*, eds. Lloyd Schwartz and Sybil P. Estess. Ann Arbor: University of Michigan Press, 1983.

LeBlanc, Suzie. *I am in need of music: Songs on Poems by Elizabeth Bishop*. Centerdiscs, 2013.

Lensing, George. "Wallace Stevens and Elizabeth Bishop: The Way a Poet Should See, The Way a Poet Should Think." *The Wallace Stevens Journal*, ed. Jacqueline Vaught Brogan, 19:2 (Fall 1995): 115–132.

Marshall, Megan. *Elizabeth Bishop: A Miracle for Breakfast*. Houghton Mifflin Harcourt, 2017.

McClatchy, J. D. *White Paper: On Contemporary Poetry*. Columbia UP, 1989.

Merrill, James. "An Interview with Donald Sheehan." *Recitative: Prose by James Merrill*, ed. J. D. McClatchy. North Point, 1986.

———. *Collected Prose*. Eds. J. D. McClatchy and Stephen Yenser. Knopf, 2004.

Millier, Brett. *Elizabeth Bishop: Life and the Memory of It*. University of California Press, 1992.

Monteiro, George, ed. *Conversations with Elizabeth Bishop*. Jackson: University Press of Mississippi, 1996.

Moore, Ben. "I am in need of music": Deborah Voigt. YouTube. https://www.youtube.com/watch?v=X4rpG80AzK4

Moore, Marianne. *Complete Prose*. Ed. Patricia Willis. Penguin, 1986.

———. *New Collected Poems*. Ed. Heather Cass White. Farrar, Straus and Giroux, 2017.

Napolitano, Marcos. "A música brasileira na década de 1950." *Revista USP* 87 (2010): 56–73.

Nowell Smith, David. *On Voice in Poetry: The Work of Animation*. Palgrave Macmillan, 2015.

Oliveira, Carmen. "O feitiço do caju." *República* (1999): 98–102.

Perelman, Bob. *The Marginalization of Poetry*. Princeton University Press, 1996.

Pronouncing Dictionary of American English, G. & C. Merriam, 1949. https://archive.org/details/pronouncingdicti00unse; accessed May 8, 2019.

Przybycien, Regina. *Feijão preto e diamantes: O Brasil na obra de Elizabeth Bishop*. Belo Horizonte: Editora UFMG, 2015.

Ravinthiran, Vidyan. *Elizabeth Bishop's Prosaic*. Bucknell UP, 2015.

———. "'Manuelzinho,' Brazil and Identity Politics." *Reading Elizabeth Bishop: An Edinburgh Companion*, ed. Jonathan Ellis. Edinburgh UP, 2019.

Rimbaud. *Complete Works, Selected Letters*. Ed. Wallace Fowlie. Chicago: University of Chicago Press, 1966.

Rosenbaum, Susan. "The Case of the Falling S: Elizabeth Bishop, Visual Poetry and the International Avant-Garde." *Reading Elizabeth Bishop: An Edinburgh Companion*, ed. Jonathan Ellis. Edinburgh UP, 2019: 177–193.

Starbuck, George. "'The Work!': A Conversation with Elizabeth Bishop." *Ploughshares*, 3:3–4 (Spring 1977): 11–29.

Sternberg, Ricardo. "Some Memories of Elizabeth Bishop." *Deslumbrante Dialética: o Brasil no olhar de Elizabeth Bishop*, eds. Sandra Regina Goulart Almeida, Maria Clara Versiany Galery, and Sílvia Maria de Oliveira Penna. Belo Horizonte: Faculdade de Letras, UFMG e Instituto de Ciências Humanas e Sociais, UFOP, 2012: 25–39.

Stevens, Wallace. *Collected Poems*. Faber, 2006.

Stevenson, Anne. *Five Looks at Elizabeth Bishop*. Bloodaxe, 2006.

Stewart, Susan. *Poetry and the Fate of the Senses*. University of Chicago Press, 2002.

Valéry, Paul. *Oeuvres I*. Paris: Bibliothèque de la Pléiade, Gallimard, 1957.

———. *Oeuvres II*. Paris: Bibliothèque de la Pléiade, Gallimard, 1960.

———. *Cahiers I*. Paris: Bibliothèque de la Pléiade, Gallimard, 1973.

———. *Cahiers II*. Paris: Bibliothèque de la Pléade, Gallimard, 1974.

White, Gillian. *Lyric Shame: The "Lyric" Subject of Contemporary American Poetry*. Harvard UP, 2014.

Wordsworth, William. *Selected Poems*. Ed. Stephen Gill. Penguin, 2004.

Index[1]

[1] Note: Page numbers followed by 'n' refer to notes.